58th Edition

Travel to Tampa Florida

2023
People Who Know
Publishing
Jack Ross

Forward: In this book, People Who Know Publishing will provide a travel guide of 101+ things to see, do and visit in Tampa Florida. We strive to make our guides as comprehensive and complete as possible. We publish travel guides on cities and countries all over the world. Feel free to check out our complete list of travel guides here:

People Who Know Publishing partners with local experts to produce travel guides on various locations. We differentiate ourselves from other travel books by focusing on areas not typically covered by others. Our guides include a detailed history of the location and its population. In addition to covering all of the "must see" areas of a location such as museums and local sights, we also provide up-to-date restaurant suggestions and local food traditions.

To make a request for a travel guide on a particular area or to join our email list to stay updated on travel tips from local experts sign up here: https://mailchi.mp/c74b62620b1f/travel-books

Be sure to confirm restaurants, addresses, and phone numbers as those may have changed since the book was published.

About the Author:

Jack Ross is a college student who was born in Westchester County, NY. He's an expert on the local "in the know" tips of the area and is an authority on Westchester and its towns. He's been featured in several publications including Business Insider and CNBC for his books.

During his spare time, he writes, plays tennis and golf and enjoys all water sports (including his latest favorite, the eFoil). Jack also enjoys traveling and is a food connoisseur throughout Westchester. Jack travels consistently and has been to majority of the states in the U.S.

Sign up for our email list to get inside access to the towns and places we cover!
>> https://mailchi.mp/c74b62620b1f/travel-books
>> https://mailchi.mp/c74b62620b1f/travel-books

Table of Contents

Tampa Florida

State: Florida

Population: 398,173

Ranking in U.S.: N/A

County: Hillsborough County

Founded: 1887

Tag line: N/A

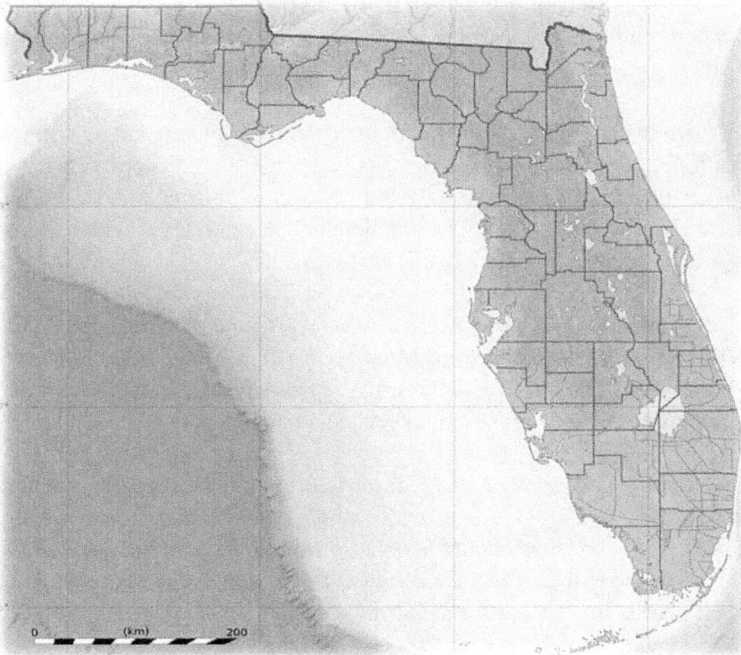

Introduction

"Florida is a fascinatingly weird place. It's kind of wild and weird, and there's a lot of experimentation happening." - Ariana Grande

Tampa, often referred to as "The Big Guava" or "The Cigar City," is a vibrant and culturally diverse city located on the western coast of the Sunshine State, Florida. Nestled along the shores of Tampa Bay and the Gulf of Mexico, Tampa is a city that seamlessly blends a rich historical past with modern innovation and a laid-back, coastal lifestyle. Known for its warm tropical climate, stunning waterfront views, and a wide range of attractions, Tampa has something to offer every visitor and resident.

With a population that reflects a mosaic of cultures, Tampa is celebrated for its multicultural festivals, delicious cuisine, and a welcoming atmosphere that embraces diversity. The city's history is deeply rooted in Cuban, Spanish, and Italian influences, which can be seen in its architecture, festivals, and culinary traditions.

Tampa is also famous for its sports culture, boasting professional teams like the Tampa Bay Buccaneers (NFL), Tampa Bay Rays (MLB), and Tampa Bay Lightning (NHL). Sports enthusiasts can enjoy year-round events and games in this sports-centric city.

The city's rich history is intertwined with industries like cigar manufacturing, which has left a lasting imprint on its heritage. Visitors can explore historic districts like Ybor City, known for its cigar heritage and vibrant nightlife, or wander through the historic neighborhoods of Hyde Park and Seminole Heights, each with its unique charm.

Beyond its historical roots, Tampa offers an array of cultural attractions, including world-class museums like the Tampa Museum of Art and the Florida Museum of Photographic Arts. The city is also home to the renowned University of South Florida, contributing to its vibrant intellectual and artistic scene.

For those seeking outdoor adventures, Tampa's proximity to beautiful beaches, such as Clearwater and St. Pete Beach, provides ample opportunities for sunbathing, water sports, and relaxation. Nature lovers can explore the nearby Everglades, go kayaking along the Hillsborough River, or visit the Florida Aquarium to learn about the diverse marine life that calls the Gulf of Mexico home.

In recent years, Tampa has experienced significant growth and development, making it an attractive destination for both tourists and residents alike. Its booming

Travel to Tampa Florida

downtown area features a riverwalk, an array of dining options, and a thriving arts and entertainment scene. Tampa International Airport serves as a major gateway to the city, connecting it with destinations worldwide.

Tampa's unique blend of history, culture, sports, and natural beauty makes it a captivating destination for those looking to experience the best that Florida's Gulf Coast has to offer. Whether you're interested in exploring its rich history, enjoying its diverse culinary scene, or simply basking in the Florida sunshine, Tampa welcomes you with open arms.

History

Spanish Exploration and Colonization:

In the early 16th century, Spanish explorers, including Ponce de León, explored the Florida peninsula, including Tampa Bay. However, it wasn't until 1521 that the Spanish established a short-lived settlement called "San Antonio de Padua" near present-day Tampa.

Seminole Wars and American Expansion:

During the early 19th century, the Seminole Wars occurred as the United States sought to remove Seminole Indians and establish control over Florida. This led to the construction of Fort Brooke, a military outpost, in 1824. It played a significant role in Tampa's early development.

Pre-European Settlement:

Before European contact, the Tampa Bay area was inhabited by various indigenous tribes, including the Tocobaga and Calusa peoples. They lived along the shores of Tampa Bay, subsisting on fishing and agriculture.

Cigar Industry and Immigrant Communities:

In the late 19th century, Tampa experienced a significant economic transformation with the growth of the cigar industry. Cuban immigrants, particularly from Key West and Havana, played a pivotal role in making Ybor City, a district within Tampa, the "Cigar Capital of the World."

The Great Fire and Rebuilding:

In 1895, a massive fire swept through Tampa, destroying much of Ybor City and causing extensive damage to the city. Despite this setback, the cigar industry rebounded, and Ybor City was rebuilt.

Civil War and Reconstruction:

During the Civil War, Tampa remained under Confederate control and served as a supply port for the Confederacy. After the war, Tampa went through a period of economic hardship during the Reconstruction era.

Urban Development and Modernization:

In the mid-20th century, Tampa underwent significant urban development and modernization. The construction of highways, bridges, and the development of suburbs contributed to the city's expansion.

Tourism and Cultural Growth:

In recent decades, Tampa has seen a surge in tourism, with attractions like Busch Gardens, the Florida Aquarium, and cultural institutions like the Tampa Museum of Art and the Straz Center for the Performing Arts enhancing the city's cultural offerings.

Sports Success:

Tampa gained prominence in the sports world with the establishment of professional sports teams such as the Tampa Bay Buccaneers (NFL), Tampa Bay Rays (MLB), and Tampa Bay Lightning (NHL). The city has hosted several Super Bowls and other major sporting events.

Economy

Finance and Business Services: Tampa is home to a growing financial and business services sector. Several major banks and financial institutions have a significant presence in the city, contributing to its reputation as a major financial hub in Florida.

Healthcare and Biotechnology: The healthcare sector is a major driver of Tampa's economy. The city is known for its world-class medical facilities, including Tampa General Hospital and Moffitt Cancer Center. Biotechnology and medical research also play a crucial role in the local economy.

Tourism and Hospitality: Tampa benefits from its proximity to popular tourist destinations, including the Gulf Coast beaches. The city attracts millions of visitors each year, supporting a thriving tourism and hospitality industry. Tampa's attractions, such as Busch Gardens, the Florida Aquarium, and cultural events, contribute to this sector's growth.

Port and Logistics: The Port of Tampa, located on Tampa Bay, is one of Florida's largest and most active deepwater ports. It handles a wide range of cargo, including bulk goods, containerized cargo, and petroleum products. The port's activities support trade, distribution, and logistics businesses in the region.

Manufacturing: Tampa has a diverse manufacturing sector, including the production of electronics, medical devices, and aerospace components. The city's proximity to major transportation routes and international markets enhances its manufacturing capabilities.

Information Technology: Tampa has been steadily growing as a hub for information technology companies, particularly in areas such as software development, data analytics, and cybersecurity.

Education: The presence of prominent educational institutions like the University of South Florida (USF) contributes to Tampa's economy. These institutions support research, education, and the development of a highly skilled workforce.

Transportation Systems

Tampa has an extensive road network, including major highways like Interstate 4 (I-4), Interstate 75 (I-75), and Interstate 275 (I-275). These highways connect Tampa to other major cities in Florida and the southeastern United States.

Hillsborough Area Regional Transit Authority (HART): HART provides bus services throughout Hillsborough County, including Tampa. It offers a network of local and express routes to help residents and commuters get around the city and its suburbs.

Tampa International Airport is one of the busiest airports in Florida and serves as a major gateway for domestic and international travelers. It offers a wide range of flights to various destinations and is known for its efficient and passenger-friendly facilities.

The Port of Tampa, located on Tampa Bay, is one of Florida's largest and most active deepwater ports. It handles a diverse range of cargo, including containers, bulk cargo, and petroleum products. The port plays a crucial role in the region's trade and transportation infrastructure.

The TECO Line Streetcar System operates a historic streetcar line that connects downtown Tampa with the historic Ybor City district. It provides a convenient and nostalgic mode of transportation for both tourists and locals.
Cycling and Pedestrian Infrastructure:

Tampa has been working to improve cycling and pedestrian infrastructure with the development of bike lanes, sidewalks, and multi-use paths. Initiatives like the Tampa Riverwalk offer a scenic route for walking and cycling along the Hillsborough River.

Tampa Bay is crisscrossed by several bridges that connect Tampa to neighboring areas. Notable bridges include the Sunshine Skyway Bridge, the Howard Frankland Bridge, and the Courtney Campbell Causeway

Ride-sharing services like Uber and Lyft operate in Tampa, providing convenient options for on-demand transportation. Traditional taxi services are also available.

.

Neighborhoods

Downtown Tampa: The heart of the city, Downtown Tampa is a bustling urban center with skyscrapers, cultural attractions, and waterfront views. It includes districts like Channel District, where you'll find the Florida Aquarium and Port Tampa Bay, and the Riverwalk, a scenic promenade along the Hillsborough River.

Ybor City: Known for its rich history and vibrant nightlife, Ybor City is a historic district with cobblestone streets, cigar factories turned into shops and restaurants, and a thriving bar and music scene. It's also famous for its annual Gasparilla Pirate Festival.

Hyde Park: This upscale neighborhood features tree-lined streets, historic homes, and the charming Hyde Park Village shopping and dining area. It's known for its historic architecture and proximity to the scenic Bayshore Boulevard, which offers stunning views of the bay.

Seminole Heights: A hip and trendy neighborhood with a mix of historic bungalows and modern homes. Seminole Heights has a thriving food scene, craft breweries, and a sense of community. It's known for its eclectic and artistic atmosphere.

Westshore: Home to Tampa's business district, Westshore features upscale shopping malls, hotels, and corporate offices. It's a major commercial and financial hub, and Tampa International Airport is located here.

Davis Islands: This island neighborhood is known for its upscale homes, beautiful waterfront views, and a small-town atmosphere. It offers parks, a private airport, and the Peter O. Knight Airport.

Food

Cuban Sandwich: Tampa is famous for its Cuban sandwich, which typically consists of Cuban bread, roast pork, ham, Swiss cheese, pickles, and mustard. It's often pressed to perfection and is a local favorite.

Cuban Cuisine: In addition to Cuban sandwiches, Tampa has many Cuban restaurants serving dishes like Ropa Vieja (shredded beef), Picadillo (ground beef hash), and Yuca con Mojo (yucca with garlic sauce).

Seafood: Being located on the Gulf Coast, Tampa offers a bounty of fresh seafood. You can enjoy dishes like grouper, snapper, stone crab claws, and Tampa Bay's famous deviled crabs.

Cajun and Creole: Tampa has a Cajun and Creole influence, with restaurants serving dishes like jambalaya, gumbo, and crawfish étouffée.

Spanish and Latin American Cuisine: Tampa's Hispanic heritage is reflected in its Spanish and Latin American restaurants, offering dishes like paella, empanadas, and arroz con pollo.

Southern Comfort Food: Southern-style cuisine can be found throughout Tampa, with offerings such as fried chicken, collard greens, and biscuits with sausage gravy.

Cuban Coffee: Don't miss the opportunity to try a strong and sweet Cuban coffee, often served in small shots called "cafecito" or "colada."

Here are our ten favorite restaurant recommendations!

1.Bern's Steak House: A Tampa institution, known for its top-quality steaks, extensive wine list, and an on-site dessert room that's a must-visit.

2.Columbia Restaurant: Florida's oldest restaurant, serving Spanish and Cuban cuisine in a historic setting. Try their famous "1905 Salad" and paella.

3.Oystercatchers: Located at the Grand Hyatt Tampa Bay, this waterfront restaurant offers fresh seafood, including oysters, crab, and Gulf-caught fish, with stunning views of Tampa Bay.

4.Eddie V's Prime Seafood: A seafood and steakhouse offering a classy dining experience, with a focus on fresh seafood and hand-cut steaks.

5.La Segunda Central Bakery: Famous for its Cuban sandwiches and freshly baked Cuban bread. A Tampa classic.

6.Columbia Cafe: A more casual offshoot of the Columbia Restaurant, located on the Riverwalk, serving Cuban and Spanish dishes in a scenic setting.

7.Datz Tampa: Known for its creative comfort food, craft beers, and an extensive menu featuring everything from mac 'n' cheese dishes to burgers and brunch options.

8.Ulele: A waterfront restaurant located in a historic Tampa Heights building, offering a diverse menu featuring Native American-inspired dishes, seafood, and craft beers.

9.Maggiano's Little Italy: A chain restaurant known for its classic Italian-American dishes like lasagna, spaghetti and meatballs, and tiramisu.

10.Donatello Italian Restaurant: A classic Italian eatery known for its romantic ambiance, traditional pasta dishes, and an extensive wine list.

Nightlife

1. *Ybor City: Ybor City is renowned for its nightlife, with a wide array of bars, clubs, and entertainment options. It's particularly famous for its historic Latin dance clubs and lively atmosphere. Some popular venues include The RITZ Ybor, The Castle, and Crowbar.*

2. *SoHo (South Howard Avenue): Located in the Hyde Park neighborhood, SoHo is a popular nightlife district known for its upscale bars, restaurants, and nightlife options. It's a great place for cocktails, dancing, and socializing.*

3. *Downtown Tampa: Downtown Tampa offers a mix of upscale bars, rooftop lounges, and live music venues. Check out the Riverwalk area for scenic views and waterside dining at places like Ulele and Armature Works.*

4. *Seminole Hard Rock Hotel & Casino: If you're into gaming and entertainment, this casino complex in Tampa offers a variety of nightlife options, including bars, restaurants, and live shows.*

5. *Live Music Venues: Tampa has several venues that host live music performances. The Orpheum, The Attic at Rock Brothers Brewing Company, and Jannus Live in nearby St. Petersburg are popular choices for live music enthusiasts.*

6. *Craft Breweries: Tampa has a thriving craft beer scene, and many breweries have taprooms where you can enjoy local brews. Cigar City Brewing, Tampa Bay Brewing Company, and Coppertail Brewing Co. are just a few options.*

Local Traditions & Customs

Gasparilla Pirate Festival: Perhaps the most famous tradition in Tampa, Gasparilla is an annual pirate-themed festival held in late January or early February. The festival includes a mock pirate invasion of the city, a large parade with colorful floats, and thousands of people dressed as pirates. It's a celebration of Tampa's maritime heritage and is inspired by the legend of Jose Gaspar, a mythical pirate who supposedly operated in the area.

Cuban Sandwich Festival: Tampa is known for its Cuban sandwiches, and every year, the city hosts the Cuban Sandwich Festival, where locals and chefs compete to make the best Cuban sandwich. It's a fun and delicious celebration of this iconic Tampa dish.

Buccaneers Football: The Tampa Bay Buccaneers, or Bucs, are the city's NFL team. Attending Buccaneers games and supporting the team is a popular local tradition, especially during football season. The team's fans, known as the "Bucs Nation," are known for their passionate support.

Weeki Wachee Springs Mermaids: While not in Tampa itself, the Weeki Wachee Springs State Park, located nearby, features live mermaid shows. The tradition dates back to the 1940s and continues to be a unique and beloved attraction.

Historical Preservation: Tampa has several neighborhoods with a rich history, such as Ybor City and Hyde Park. Preserving historic buildings and cultural heritage is an important tradition in these areas, and there are efforts to maintain their unique character.

Cultural Festivals: Tampa hosts a variety of cultural festivals throughout the year, celebrating the city's diverse communities. These festivals often feature music, dance, food, and art from different cultures, fostering a sense of unity and appreciation for Tampa's multicultural heritage.

What to buy?

Cuban Sandwich: Tampa is famous for its Cuban sandwiches, so bring home some Cuban bread, Cuban roast pork, and other ingredients to recreate this iconic sandwich.

Cigars: Ybor City, a historic district in Tampa, has a long history of cigar manufacturing. You can buy hand-rolled cigars from local cigar shops as well as cigar-related accessories.

Hot Sauce: Florida is known for its spicy cuisine, and Tampa is no exception. Look for locally made hot sauces and spice blends to add some heat to your dishes.

Craft Beer: Tampa has a thriving craft beer scene. Visit local breweries and bring home some of their unique brews or merchandise like T-shirts and glassware.

Seafood: Florida's Gulf Coast is known for its fresh seafood. Consider buying some local specialties like stone crab claws, smoked fish, or fish dip.

Art and Crafts: Explore local art galleries and craft markets for unique pieces of art, pottery, jewelry, and other handmade goods created by Tampa's talented artists.

Gourmet Foods: Look for gourmet foods like key lime pie, Datil pepper products, and locally produced honey and preserves at specialty food stores and markets.

Finally, here are the five most famous people from the city!

1.Derek Jeter: The legendary former New York Yankees shortstop and Major League Baseball (MLB) star, Derek Jeter, was born in Pequannock Township, New Jersey, but he spent much of his childhood and adolescence in Tampa. He is considered one of the greatest baseball players of all time and is known for his leadership on and off the field.

2.Hulk Hogan (Terry Bollea): The iconic professional wrestler Hulk Hogan has strong ties to the Tampa Bay area. He is a multiple-time world champion and was a key figure in the wrestling boom of the 1980s and 1990s.

3.Brooke and Nick Hogan: The children of Hulk Hogan, Brooke Hogan is a singer, actress, and media personality, while Nick Hogan is known for his appearances on reality TV shows and his involvement in motorsports.

4.John Cena: While born in West Newbury, Massachusetts, professional wrestler and actor John Cena resides in the Tampa Bay area. Cena is a WWE superstar known for his philanthropic efforts and has transitioned into a successful acting career.

5.Steve Garvey: Former MLB first baseman Steve Garvey, best known for his time with the Los Angeles Dodgers and San Diego Padres, was born in Tampa. He is a ten-time All-Star and a World Series champion.

101+ things to do in the city

1. Visit Busch Gardens Tampa Bay.
2. Take a stroll along the Tampa Riverwalk.
3. Explore the Tampa Bay History Center.
4. Attend a Tampa Bay Buccaneers game.
5. Relax at Clearwater Beach.
6. Visit the Florida Aquarium.
7. Explore Ybor City's historic district.
8. Go fishing in Tampa Bay.
9. Enjoy a Cuban sandwich at the Columbia Restaurant.
10. Go paddleboarding on the Hillsborough River.
11. Watch a Tampa Bay Lightning hockey game.
12. Take a scenic drive along Bayshore Boulevard.
13. Visit the Tampa Museum of Art.
14. Try Cuban coffee at a local cafe.
15. Explore the Tampa Bay Performing Arts Center.
16. Go birdwatching at Lettuce Lake Regional Park.
17. Visit the University of South Florida Botanical Gardens.
18. Take a cruise on the StarShip Dining Yacht.
19. Explore the Henry B. Plant Museum at the University of Tampa.
20. Go kayaking in Tampa's waterways.
21. Attend a live concert at Amalie Arena.
22. Visit the Glazer Children's Museum.
23. Explore the Tampa Bay Watch Discovery Center.
24. Explore the historic Hyde Park Village shopping district.
25. Take a day trip to Honeymoon Island State Park.
26. Experience the Gasparilla Pirate Festival.
27. Try stand-up paddleboarding in Tampa Bay.
28. Visit the Lowry Park Zoo.
29. Explore the Tampa Theatre.
30. Go snorkeling in the Gulf of Mexico.
31. Attend a Tampa Bay Rays baseball game.
32. Take a scenic sunset cruise.
33. Visit Big Cat Rescue.
34. Try jet skiing on the bay.
35. Explore the Manatee Viewing Center.
36. Go on a wildlife safari.
37. Visit the Salvador Dali Museum in nearby St. Petersburg.
38. Attend a Tampa Bay Rowdies soccer game.
39. Go on a ghost tour of Ybor City.
40. Visit the Tampa Bay Downs racetrack.

41. Explore the Museum of Science and Industry (MOSI).
42. Go on a Tampa Bay brewery tour.
43. Attend the Florida State Fair.
44. Visit the SS American Victory Mariners' Memorial and Museum Ship.
45. Explore the International Plaza and Bay Street shopping mall.
46. Go hiking in Brooker Creek Preserve.
47. Visit the Leepa-Rattner Museum of Art in Tarpon Springs.
48. Take a scenic flightseeing tour.
49. Explore the Sulphur Springs Museum and Heritage Center.
50. Go deep-sea fishing in the Gulf of Mexico.
51. Visit the Tampa Bay Automobile Museum.
52. Attend a Tampa Bay Storm arena football game.
53. Explore Lettuce Lake Park.
54. Take a scenic drive to Tarpon Springs.
55. Visit the Tampa Bay Downs Golf Practice Facility.
56. Attend the Gasparilla Music Festival.
57. Go camping at Fort De Soto Park.
58. Visit the Tampa Bay Firefighters Museum.
59. Explore the Tampa Bay Watch Bay Discovery Center.
60. Attend the Tampa Bay International Dragon Boat Races.
61. Go on a Segway tour of Tampa.
62. Visit the Upper Tampa Bay Trail.
63. Attend the Tampa Bay Black Heritage Festival.
64. Explore the Channel District.
65. Go on a casino cruise.
66. Attend the Tampa International Gay and Lesbian Film Festival.
67. Visit the Tampa Bay Aviation Association.
68. Go on a brewery bike tour.
69. Explore the Curtis Hixon Waterfront Park.
70. Attend the Tampa Greek Festival.
71. Visit the American Victory Ship Mariners' Memorial Museum.
72. Go on a sunset hot air balloon ride.
73. Explore Fort Foster State Historic Site.
74. Visit the Tampa Bay Automobile Museum.
75. Go on a Tampa Bay food tour.
76. Attend the Tampa Pig Jig.
77. Explore the Upper Tampa Bay Trail.
78. Visit the Tampa Baseball Museum at the Al Lopez House.
79. Attend a Tampa Roller Derby match.
80. Explore Old Tampa Bay.
81. Go on a wildlife eco-tour.

82. Visit the Florida Southern College campus in nearby Lakeland.
83. Attend the Tampa Bay Improv Festival.
84. Explore the historic Hyde Park Village shopping district.
85. Go on a Tampa Bay ghost hunting tour.
86. Visit the Tampa Port Authority.
87. Attend the Tampa International Fringe Festival.
88. Explore Ballast Point Park.
89. Go on a Tampa Bay fishing charter.
90. Visit the Tampa Bay Estuary Program.
91. Attend the Tampa Bay Comic Con.
92. Explore the Westchase Golf Club.
93. Go on a paddleboard yoga session.
94. Visit the Tampa Bay Performing Arts Center.
95. Attend a Tampa Bay Roller Derby match.
96. Explore the Veterans Memorial Park and Museum.
97. Go on a Tampa Bay brewery crawl.
98. Visit the Tampa Bay Downs Golf Practice Facility.
99. Attend the Gasparilla International Film Festival.
100. Explore the Upper Tampa Bay Conservation Park.
101. Go on a guided bike tour of Tampa.
102. Visit the Tampa Bay Area Renaissance Festival.
103. Attend a Tampa Bay Rowdies soccer game.
104. Explore the Florida Holocaust Museum in nearby St. Petersburg.
105. Go on a Tampa Bay wildlife photography tour.
106. Visit the Tampa Bay Automobile Museum.
107. Go on a Tampa Bay Segway tour.
108. Explore the Ballast Point Park and Pier.
109. Go on a fishing excursion in Tampa Bay.
110. Visit the Glazer Children's Museum.

1.Visit Busch Gardens Tampa Bay.

Busch Gardens Tampa Bay is a world-renowned theme park located in Tampa, Florida. It's known for its thrilling rides, exciting animal encounters, live entertainment, and beautiful landscaping. Here's an overview of what you can expect when visiting Busch Gardens Tampa Bay:

Rides and Attractions: Busch Gardens Tampa Bay offers a wide range of rides and attractions to cater to visitors of all ages. Some of the most famous rides include SheiKra, a dive coaster with a 200-foot drop, Cheetah Hunt, a high-speed roller coaster, and Montu, an inverted roller coaster with seven inversions. There are also family-friendly rides and attractions like the Serengeti Safari and the Congo River Rapids.

Animal Experiences: One of the unique aspects of Busch Gardens Tampa Bay is its focus on wildlife conservation and education. You can get up close and personal with a variety of animals, including giraffes, zebras, kangaroos, and more. The park has themed animal habitats that mimic the natural environments of these creatures, allowing for an immersive experience.

Live Shows: Busch Gardens offers a variety of live shows and entertainment options throughout the day. These shows feature talented performers, such as acrobats, musicians, and animal trainers, providing entertainment and education for visitors.

Dining and Shopping: The park offers a range of dining options, from quick-service eateries to sit-down restaurants. You can sample a variety of cuisines, including barbecue, Asian, and Mediterranean. There are also numerous shops where you can purchase souvenirs, clothing, and unique gifts.

Seasonal Events: Busch Gardens hosts special events and festivals throughout the year, such as Howl-O-Scream for Halloween and Christmas Town during the holiday season. These events feature themed decorations, entertainment, and activities.

Water Rides: On hot Florida days, you can cool off on water rides like Stanley Falls Flume and Congo River Rapids. These rides offer a refreshing break from the Florida heat.

Children's Activities: Busch Gardens is family-friendly and provides a variety of activities for younger visitors, including play areas, animal encounters, and rides designed for children.

Conservation: The park is committed to wildlife conservation and often participates in breeding and rescue programs. Visitors can learn about these efforts and the importance of protecting endangered species.

Scenic Landscaping: Busch Gardens Tampa Bay is known for its beautiful landscaping, with lush gardens, water features, and scenic views. It provides a pleasant and immersive environment for guests to enjoy.

Thrill-Seeking Experiences: If you're an adrenaline junkie, Busch Gardens Tampa Bay offers some of the most thrilling rides in Florida, including some of the tallest and fastest roller coasters in the state.

Busch Gardens Tampa Bay offers a unique combination of thrilling rides, animal encounters, and educational experiences, making it a popular destination for families and adventure seekers alike.

2. Take a stroll along the Tampa Riverwalk.

Taking a stroll along the Tampa Riverwalk is a delightful way to explore the heart of downtown Tampa while enjoying the scenic beauty of the Hillsborough River. Here's what you can expect when you embark on this leisurely walk:

Scenic Views: The Tampa Riverwalk offers picturesque views of the Hillsborough River, which flows through downtown Tampa. You'll enjoy tranquil waters, lush greenery, and the city skyline as your backdrop.

Waterfront Parks: Along the way, you'll pass by several waterfront parks and green spaces. These parks provide opportunities for picnicking, relaxation, and taking in the natural surroundings.

Public Art: The Riverwalk features a variety of public art installations, sculptures, and murals that add artistic flair to your stroll. Keep an eye out for these creative works as you walk.

Historical Landmarks: You'll encounter historical landmarks and markers that provide insights into Tampa's rich history and cultural heritage. These include interpretive signs and plaques.

Dining and Refreshments: The Riverwalk is lined with restaurants, cafes, and food vendors, making it easy to stop for a meal, snack, or refreshing beverage as you walk. Many of these establishments offer outdoor seating with lovely river views.

Biking and Jogging: In addition to walking, the Riverwalk provides dedicated lanes for biking and jogging, allowing for various forms of recreation and exercise.

River Activities: Depending on the time of day and season, you may see kayakers, paddleboarders, and other water enthusiasts enjoying the river. Some areas offer kayak rentals if you'd like to try it for yourself.

Cultural Stops: The Riverwalk connects to several cultural attractions, including the Tampa Bay History Center, the Florida Aquarium, and the Tampa Museum of Art. You can make stops along the way to explore these institutions.

Events and Festivals: The Riverwalk often hosts events, festivals, and live performances. Check the event calendar to see if any special happenings align with your visit.

Sunsets: The Riverwalk is an excellent spot to catch a breathtaking sunset over the Hillsborough River. Many visitors and locals gather here in the evenings to watch the sun dip below the horizon.

Relaxation and Serenity: The overall ambiance of the Riverwalk is serene and inviting. It's a place to escape the hustle and bustle of the city and find a sense of peace by the water.

Photography Opportunities: Whether you're an amateur or professional photographer, the Tampa Riverwalk provides a myriad of scenic and architectural subjects to capture through your lens.

The Tampa Riverwalk is not only a pleasant stroll but also an opportunity to immerse yourself in the natural beauty and cultural vibrancy of downtown Tampa. It's a must-do activity for visitors and a favorite pastime for locals looking to connect with the city's waterfront charm.

3.Explore the Tampa Bay History Center.

The Tampa Bay History Center is a fascinating museum located in downtown Tampa, Florida, dedicated to preserving and showcasing the rich history and cultural heritage of the Tampa Bay region. Here's what you can expect when you explore this museum:

Historical Exhibits: The Tampa Bay History Center features a wide range of engaging exhibits that chronicle the history of the Tampa Bay area, from its Native American inhabitants to the present day. The exhibits are well-curated and provide a comprehensive look at the region's past.

Interactive Displays: Many of the exhibits are interactive, allowing visitors of all ages to engage with the history in a hands-on way. You can explore artifacts, photographs, and multimedia presentations that bring the past to life.

Native American History: Learn about the indigenous peoples who inhabited the Tampa Bay area long before European settlers arrived. The museum's exhibits delve into the history, culture, and contributions of Native American communities.

Pioneer Days: Discover what life was like for the early pioneers who settled in the Tampa Bay region. You can explore exhibits about homesteading, the cigar industry, and the development of the city.

Cigar Industry: Tampa has a rich history in the cigar industry, and the museum highlights the impact of this industry on the city's development. You'll learn about the legacy of cigar manufacturing in Ybor City.

Civil War and Military History: Explore exhibits related to the American Civil War and the role that Tampa played during this period. Additionally, the museum covers military history, including the Spanish-American War and the World Wars.

Maritime History: Tampa's connection to the sea is a significant part of its history. You can see exhibits related to shipbuilding, the port, and the maritime industry that shaped the city.

Sports and Entertainment: The museum also features displays on Tampa's sports history, including the Tampa Bay Buccaneers and the Tampa Bay Lightning. You can also learn about the region's contributions to the world of entertainment.

Temporary Exhibitions: In addition to its permanent exhibits, the Tampa Bay History Center hosts rotating temporary exhibitions that cover a wide range of topics, ensuring there's something new to discover during each visit.

Educational Programs: The museum offers educational programs and events for visitors of all ages, including lectures, workshops, and guided tours. It's a great place to learn and engage with local history.

Waterfront Location: The Tampa Bay History Center is situated along the waterfront, providing beautiful views of the Hillsborough River and the Channelside district. The building itself is a modern architectural gem.

Museum Store: Before you leave, be sure to visit the museum store, where you can find a variety of books, gifts, and souvenirs related to Tampa's history and culture.

The Tampa Bay History Center is not only an educational experience but also a celebration of the diverse and dynamic history of the Tampa Bay area. It's an excellent destination for history enthusiasts, families, and anyone interested in learning more about the region's past.

4.Attend a Tampa Bay Buccaneers game.

Attending a Tampa Bay Buccaneers game is an exhilarating experience for football fans and a great way to immerse yourself in the excitement of the NFL. Here's what you can expect when you attend a Buccaneers game at Raymond James Stadium:

Game Day Atmosphere: Game days in Tampa are filled with excitement and anticipation. The atmosphere around the stadium is electric, with fans tailgating, wearing team colors, and getting into the spirit of the game.

Raymond James Stadium: The Buccaneers play their home games at Raymond James Stadium, a state-of-the-art facility known for its unique design and comfortable amenities. It's often referred to as "Ray Jay" by fans.

Tailgating: Tailgating is a popular pre-game tradition in Tampa. Fans gather in the parking lots surrounding the stadium to grill food, enjoy beverages, and socialize with fellow Buccaneers supporters.

Buccaneers Merchandise: Before entering the stadium, you'll find plenty of vendors selling Buccaneers merchandise, including jerseys, hats, foam fingers, and more. It's an opportunity to deck yourself out in team gear.

Food and Beverages: Inside the stadium, you'll have access to a variety of food and beverage options. Enjoy classic game-day fare like hot dogs, nachos, and pretzels, as well as local favorites.

Buccaneers Marching Band and Cheerleaders: Be entertained by the spirited performances of the Tampa Bay Buccaneers' marching band and cheerleaders, who provide entertainment throughout the game.

Jumbotron and Entertainment: Raymond James Stadium features a massive Jumbotron screen that provides close-up views of the action, as well as entertaining content during breaks in the game.

National Anthem: The singing of the national anthem is a moving and patriotic moment before the game begins. It's a time for fans to show their respect and pride.

Halftime Show: Enjoy the halftime show, which often features live music performances, dance routines, or special presentations.

Camaraderie: Attending a Buccaneers game is an opportunity to bond with fellow fans, share in the ups and downs of the game, and create lasting memories with friends and family.

Player Introductions: Witness the excitement as the players are introduced onto the field, including the legendary pirate ship at one end of the stadium.

Touchdown Celebrations: When the Buccaneers score a touchdown, the crowd erupts with cheers and excitement. Celebrate with fellow fans as you watch the team's celebratory rituals.

Game-Winning Moments: Whether it's a last-minute touchdown, a crucial interception, or a game-winning field goal, the moments of victory are unforgettable and shared by fans as they celebrate together.

Interact with the Pirate Ship: The iconic pirate ship inside Raymond James Stadium comes to life with cannons firing and fans chanting "Fire the cannons!" when the Buccaneers score.

Post-Game Reactions: After the game, you can join the crowd in discussing the highlights, reliving the action, and sharing your thoughts on the game's outcome.

Attending a Tampa Bay Buccaneers game is a thrilling experience filled with camaraderie, excitement, and memorable moments. Whether you're a die-hard fan or just looking for a fun day out, it's an event that captures the essence of American football culture.

5.Relax at Clearwater Beach.

Relaxing at Clearwater Beach is a quintessential Florida experience, offering sun, sand, and a laid-back atmosphere. Here's what you can expect when you visit this beautiful Gulf Coast beach:

Glistening White Sand: Clearwater Beach is renowned for its soft, powdery white sand. The beach's pristine sands are perfect for sunbathing, building sandcastles, or simply taking a leisurely walk along the shoreline.

Crystal-Clear Waters: The Gulf of Mexico's waters at Clearwater Beach are known for their clarity and inviting warmth. They're ideal for swimming, wading, and enjoying water activities.

Beachfront Accommodations: Clearwater Beach offers a variety of beachfront hotels and resorts, making it easy to stay close to the shore and enjoy stunning views of the Gulf.

Sunbathing: Whether you prefer lounging on a towel, a beach chair, or a rented cabana, you can soak up the sun's rays while listening to the soothing sound of the waves.

Water Activities: Clearwater Beach offers a range of water sports and activities, including parasailing, jet skiing, paddleboarding, and dolphin-watching tours. There are rental shops and tour operators along the beach.

Pier 60: Visit Pier 60, which extends into the Gulf and is a hub of activity. You can find shops, vendors, street performers, and daily sunset celebrations at this lively spot.

Shelling: Clearwater Beach is a great place for shell collecting, particularly in the early morning. You may find beautiful seashells as you stroll along the shore.

Beachfront Dining: Enjoy a meal or a refreshing drink at one of the beachfront restaurants and bars. Many offer outdoor seating with panoramic views of the Gulf.

Beach Volleyball: Look for beach volleyball courts and join in a game with friends or fellow visitors. It's a fun way to stay active on the beach.

Sunset Views: Clearwater Beach is famous for its stunning sunsets over the Gulf of Mexico. Be sure to stay until evening to witness the breathtaking colors as the sun dips below the horizon.

Family-Friendly: Clearwater Beach is family-friendly, with gentle waves and a relaxed atmosphere. It's a safe and enjoyable destination for families with children.

Beachfront Entertainment: Depending on the season, you might find live music, festivals, and other entertainment events taking place along the beach, providing additional fun and excitement.

Fishing: If you enjoy fishing, you can cast your line from the pier or take a fishing charter to explore deeper waters.

Nature Walks: Clearwater Beach is part of a barrier island, and there are opportunities for nature walks and birdwatching in nearby natural areas and parks.

Relaxation: Most importantly, Clearwater Beach offers a serene and tranquil environment where you can unwind, read a book, or simply enjoy the peacefulness of the Gulf Coast.

Clearwater Beach is often ranked as one of the top beaches in the United States, and it's easy to see why. Whether you're seeking adventure or relaxation, it offers a wide range of experiences for visitors of all ages, making it a popular destination on Florida's west coast.

6. Visit the Florida Aquarium.

Visiting the Florida Aquarium in Tampa is an educational and entertaining experience for all ages. Here's what you can expect when you explore this renowned aquarium:

Exhibits: The Florida Aquarium features a variety of immersive and informative exhibits that showcase the diverse aquatic ecosystems of Florida and beyond. These exhibits include the Wetlands Trail, Coral Reef, Bays and Beaches, Ocean Commotion, and the Journey to Madagascar.

Native Florida Wildlife: Discover the unique flora and fauna of Florida's waterways, including alligators, otters, seahorses, and various species of fish and birds. The Wetlands Trail exhibit allows you to explore a replica of Florida's wetlands and mangrove forests.

Coral Reefs: The Coral Reef exhibit transports you to a vibrant and colorful underwater world, complete with live coral, tropical fish, and even sharks. It provides insights into the importance of coral reefs and their conservation.

Marine Life Conservation: The Florida Aquarium is dedicated to marine life conservation and education. You'll learn about their efforts to protect and preserve endangered species and their habitats.

Touch Tanks: Get hands-on with marine life in the touch tanks, where you can interact with stingrays, sea stars, and other aquatic creatures. It's a fun and educational experience for visitors of all ages.

Interactive Displays: Throughout the aquarium, you'll find interactive displays and informational panels that provide insights into marine biology, ecology, and conservation efforts.

Aquatic Adventures: The Florida Aquarium offers unique experiences like behind-the-scenes tours, dive with the sharks programs, and animal encounters, allowing you to get up close with some of the marine residents.

Outdoor Play Area: If you're visiting with children, the outdoor play area provides a place for kids to burn off energy while still enjoying water-related activities.

Educational Programs: The aquarium offers educational programs and workshops for visitors of all ages, making it a great destination for school groups and families looking to learn about marine life.

Conservation and Research: Learn about the important research and conservation work being conducted by the Florida Aquarium to protect marine environments and species.

Dining Options: The on-site cafeteria and snack bar offer a variety of food and beverage options, so you can enjoy a meal or a snack during your visit.

Gift Shop: The aquarium's gift shop offers a wide range of marine-themed souvenirs, gifts, and educational materials to remember your visit.

Community Events: Throughout the year, the Florida Aquarium hosts special events, including themed parties, family nights, and conservation-focused activities.

Beautiful Views: The aquarium's location on the waterfront provides stunning views of the surrounding area and Tampa Bay, making it a picturesque destination.

Accessibility: The Florida Aquarium is wheelchair accessible and strives to provide a comfortable and enjoyable experience for all visitors.

Visiting the Florida Aquarium is not only an opportunity to see incredible marine life but also a chance to gain a deeper understanding of the importance of conserving our oceans and aquatic ecosystems. It's a memorable and educational experience that combines entertainment with environmental awareness.

7.Explore Ybor City's historic district.

Exploring Ybor City is a captivating journey into the rich history and vibrant culture of this historic district in Tampa, Florida. Here's what you can expect when you visit Ybor City:

Historical Significance: Ybor City is known for its historical significance as the "Cigar Capital of the World." It was established in the late 19th century by cigar manufacturers and cigar workers, many of whom were immigrants from Cuba, Spain, and Italy.

Architecture: The district features well-preserved historic architecture with colorful buildings, iron balconies, and brick streets. The architecture reflects the influence of the various immigrant groups that settled here.

Centennial Park: Start your exploration at Centennial Park, a central gathering place in Ybor City. It often hosts events, festivals, and outdoor performances, making it a hub of activity.

Ybor City State Museum: Visit the Ybor City State Museum to learn about the history of the district. The museum offers informative exhibits on the cigar industry, immigrant communities, and Ybor City's cultural heritage.

Cigar Heritage: Ybor City is renowned for its cigar heritage. Explore the historic cigar factories, shops, and boutiques, and learn about the art of cigar making.

Cuban Influence: Experience the Cuban influence in Ybor City by trying Cuban coffee at a local cafe, enjoying Cuban sandwiches at a restaurant, or exploring the Cuban Club, a social and cultural center.

Shopping: Ybor City offers unique shopping opportunities, including boutiques, art galleries, and shops selling cigars, Latin American crafts, and vintage items.

Nightlife: Ybor City comes alive at night with a vibrant nightlife scene. Explore the bars, clubs, and live music venues for a taste of Tampa's nightlife.

Dining: Sample diverse cuisines, from Cuban and Spanish to Italian and Colombian, at the district's many restaurants. Don't miss the opportunity to try a hearty Spanish paella.

Historic Landmarks: Visit landmarks like the Ybor City Historic Cigar Museum, the Columbia Restaurant (Florida's oldest restaurant), and the Italian Club of Tampa.

Art and Murals: Ybor City boasts an array of colorful murals and street art that add to the district's charm. Take a walking tour to discover these artistic gems.

Galleries: Explore art galleries showcasing local and international artists. The district has a thriving arts community.

Events and Festivals: Ybor City hosts numerous events and festivals throughout the year, including the Gasparilla Festival and the Ybor City Art Walk. Check the event calendar for upcoming festivities.

Historical Tours: Consider taking a guided historical tour of Ybor City to gain deeper insights into its past and cultural significance.

Transportation: Ybor City is easily accessible from downtown Tampa and other parts of the city. You can explore the district on foot or take a streetcar ride from downtown.

Ybor City's historic district is a vibrant and culturally rich neighborhood that offers a unique blend of history, art, cuisine, and entertainment. It's a must-visit destination for those interested in Tampa's diverse heritage and lively atmosphere

8.Go fishing in Tampa Bay.

Fishing in Tampa Bay is a popular and rewarding activity for both novice and experienced anglers. Tampa Bay offers a variety of fishing opportunities, from freshwater to saltwater, and provides a chance to catch a wide range of fish species. Here's what you can expect when you go fishing in Tampa Bay:

Abundant Fish Species: Tampa Bay is home to an abundance of fish species, including redfish, snook, trout, tarpon, snapper, grouper, mackerel, and more. Depending on the season and location, you can target specific species.

Fishing Charters: Numerous fishing charters and guides operate in Tampa Bay. These experienced captains can take you to the best fishing spots, provide equipment, and offer valuable expertise to increase your chances of success.

Inshore and Offshore Fishing: Tampa Bay offers both inshore and offshore fishing opportunities. Inshore fishing is popular for redfish, snook, and trout, while offshore trips target larger species like grouper and snapper.

Fly Fishing: Fly fishing enthusiasts can enjoy the shallow flats and backwaters of Tampa Bay, where you can stalk redfish and snook using fly rods.

Shore Fishing: If you prefer fishing from land, there are many parks, piers, and shoreline spots where you can cast your line into the bay. Fort De Soto Park, Ballast Point Park, and the Skyway Fishing Pier State Park are popular options.

Catch and Release: Many anglers practice catch and release to conserve fish populations. It's essential to be aware of local regulations regarding catch limits and size restrictions.

Fishing Tournaments: Tampa Bay hosts various fishing tournaments and competitions throughout the year. These events often attract anglers from all over the region.

Bait and Tackle Shops: You'll find numerous bait and tackle shops in the Tampa Bay area where you can purchase bait, fishing gear, and other supplies.

Fishing Seasons: Some fish species in Tampa Bay have specific seasons when they are more abundant or legally catchable. Check local regulations and fishing calendars for the best times to target your preferred species.

Scenic Views: While fishing, you'll have the opportunity to enjoy the scenic beauty of Tampa Bay, including its natural landscapes, birdlife, and occasional dolphin sightings.

Licensing: Ensure you have the appropriate fishing license, which can be obtained from the Florida Fish and Wildlife Conservation Commission website or local licensing agents.

Weather Considerations: Be mindful of Florida's weather conditions, which can change rapidly. It's a good idea to check the weather forecast and be prepared for sun, rain, or wind.

Respect for Wildlife: Practice ethical and responsible fishing by respecting wildlife and the environment. Dispose of trash properly and follow guidelines for safe handling and release of fish.

Fishing in Tampa Bay offers not only the excitement of reeling in a catch but also the opportunity to enjoy the beauty of the bay's surroundings. Whether you're an angling enthusiast or a beginner looking for a memorable outdoor experience, Tampa Bay provides a diverse and rewarding fishing environment.

9.Enjoy a Cuban sandwich at the Columbia Restaurant.

Indulging in a Cuban sandwich at the Columbia Restaurant is a culinary delight and a cultural experience in Tampa, Florida. Here's what you can expect when you enjoy this iconic Cuban sandwich at the historic Columbia Restaurant:

Travel to Tampa Florida

Historic Ambiance: The Columbia Restaurant is one of the oldest and most iconic dining establishments in Florida. Founded in 1905, it exudes historic charm and ambiance, with ornate decor and a rich history.

Signature Dish: The Columbia's Cuban sandwich is renowned for its delicious combination of flavors. It typically consists of roast pork, ham, Swiss cheese, pickles, and mustard, all pressed between Cuban bread. The result is a mouthwatering, savory, and slightly tangy sandwich.

Variations: While the classic Cuban sandwich is a staple, the Columbia Restaurant offers a few variations that may include additional ingredients like salami or Genoa ham. You can choose the one that suits your taste.

Fresh Ingredients: The Columbia Restaurant prides itself on using high-quality, fresh ingredients to create their Cuban sandwiches, ensuring a satisfying and flavorful experience.

Sides and Accompaniments: Enjoy your Cuban sandwich with a side of Spanish bean soup, black beans and rice, or their famous "1905" salad, which features iceberg lettuce, baked ham, Swiss cheese, olives, and a secret dressing.

Outdoor Dining: Depending on the location, you may have the option to dine al fresco, allowing you to savor your Cuban sandwich while enjoying the Florida sunshine and a pleasant ambiance.

Live Entertainment: Some Columbia Restaurant locations offer live entertainment in the evenings, including flamenco dancing and Spanish guitar performances, adding to the overall dining experience.

Historic Locations: The Columbia Restaurant has multiple locations, including the flagship location in Tampa's Ybor City historic district. Each location carries its own unique charm and history.

Cultural Heritage: Dining at the Columbia Restaurant provides a glimpse into the rich cultural heritage of Tampa and the influence of Cuban and Spanish cuisine on the region.

Friendly Service: Expect attentive and friendly service from the restaurant's staff, who are known for their hospitality.

Reservations: As the Columbia Restaurant is a popular dining destination, it's a good idea to make reservations, especially during peak dining hours or on weekends.

Desserts: Don't forget to save room for dessert! The restaurant offers a tempting selection of Spanish and Cuban desserts, such as flan and churros.

Takeout: If you're on the go or prefer to enjoy your Cuban sandwich elsewhere, the Columbia Restaurant may offer takeout options so you can savor this classic sandwich wherever you like.

Whether you're a local or a visitor to Tampa, enjoying a Cuban sandwich at the Columbia Restaurant is a delectable and culturally enriching experience that pays homage to the culinary traditions of the region.

10.Go paddleboarding on the Hillsborough River.

Paddleboarding on the Hillsborough River in Tampa is a serene and scenic way to explore the natural beauty of the area while enjoying outdoor recreation. Here's what you can expect when you go paddleboarding on the Hillsborough River:

Rentals and Equipment: Start by renting a paddleboard from one of the local outfitters or rental shops in the Tampa area. They typically provide paddleboards, paddles, life vests, and basic instructions if you're new to paddleboarding.

Scenic River Views: As you paddle along the Hillsborough River, you'll be treated to beautiful and peaceful surroundings. The river is lined with lush vegetation, including mangroves, cypress trees, and a variety of wildlife.

Wildlife Viewing: Keep an eye out for wildlife during your paddleboarding adventure. You might spot birds like herons, egrets, ospreys, and maybe even an occasional manatee or dolphin in the river.

Natural Springs: Some sections of the Hillsborough River are known for natural springs that provide crystal-clear water and a refreshing break from the Florida heat. Cypress Point Park and Lettuce Lake Park are popular spots for exploring these springs.

Tranquil Environment: Paddleboarding offers a quiet and tranquil experience on the water. It's an opportunity to disconnect from the hustle and bustle of daily life and connect with nature.

Beginner-Friendly: Paddleboarding is a beginner-friendly water activity. Even if you're new to it, the calm waters of the Hillsborough River make it a suitable place to learn the ropes.

Exercise and Relaxation: Paddleboarding provides an excellent full-body workout as you use your core, arms, and legs to paddle. It's also a relaxing and meditative activity, allowing you to unwind and enjoy the outdoors.

Paddling Options: Depending on your preferences, you can choose to paddle downstream, upstream, or explore calm tributaries and coves along the river. There are routes suitable for all skill levels.

Safety First: Remember to wear a life vest or personal flotation device while paddleboarding. Safety should always be a priority when participating in water sports.

Sun Protection: Florida's sun can be intense, so apply sunscreen, wear a hat, and bring sunglasses to protect yourself from the sun's rays.

Respect Nature: When paddleboarding on the Hillsborough River, practice responsible eco-tourism by not disturbing wildlife or damaging the river's ecosystem. Leave no trace and help preserve the natural environment.

Guided Tours: If you're looking for a guided experience, consider joining a guided paddleboarding tour. Experienced guides can provide insights into the local ecology and history.

Paddleboarding on the Hillsborough River offers a unique perspective of Tampa's natural beauty and is a great way to enjoy the outdoors. Whether you're seeking a peaceful and reflective journey or an active workout on the water, this activity provides a memorable and scenic experience.

11.Watch a Tampa Bay Lightning hockey game.

Watching a Tampa Bay Lightning hockey game is an exciting and high-energy experience for sports fans. The Lightning are a professional ice hockey team based in Tampa, Florida, and they compete in the National Hockey League (NHL). Here's what you can expect when you attend a Tampa Bay Lightning game:

Amalie Arena: The Lightning play their home games at the Amalie Arena, a modern and state-of-the-art facility located in downtown Tampa. The arena offers excellent seating, amenities, and a lively atmosphere.

Game Day Atmosphere: Game days at the Amalie Arena are filled with excitement and enthusiasm. Fans, known as the "Bolts Nation," gather to support their team, creating a spirited and electric atmosphere.

Tampa Bay Lightning Merchandise: Before the game, explore the team store and various merchandise stands inside the arena to get your hands on Lightning jerseys, hats, t-shirts, and other memorabilia to show your team spirit.

Food and Beverage Options: The Amalie Arena offers a wide range of food and beverage options, including traditional game-day fare like hot dogs, nachos, and popcorn. You can also find local and international cuisines to satisfy your appetite.

Interactive Fan Zone: The arena often has an interactive fan zone where you can participate in games, activities, and photo opportunities before the game or during intermissions.

Live Entertainment: Enjoy live music performances, cheerleaders, and in-game entertainment that keep fans engaged and entertained throughout the game.

The Tesla Coil: One of the unique features of Lightning games is the Tesla coil, which produces electric sparks and creates a dramatic effect during goals and special moments.

Community Involvement: The Tampa Bay Lightning are actively involved in the local community and often host charitable events and initiatives. Supporting the team can also mean supporting worthy causes.

Lightning Strikes: Experience the excitement of "Thunder Alley" outside the arena, where fans gather to socialize, watch live broadcasts, and take part in pre-game festivities.

Chasing the Stanley Cup: The Lightning have been highly competitive in the NHL in recent years and have won the prestigious Stanley Cup. Attending a game gives you a chance to watch a championship-caliber team in action.

Game Entertainment: In addition to the hockey action, the Lightning's game production includes video highlights, player introductions, and interactive fan engagement on the arena's video screens.

Meet Thunderbug: Say hello to Thunderbug, the Lightning's mascot, who entertains fans young and old with antics and high-fives.

Interact with Fans: Join in the camaraderie and conversations with fellow fans during the game, sharing the highs and lows of each play.

Tampa Bay Lightning Foundation: Learn about the team's charitable efforts and how they give back to the Tampa Bay community.

Celebrate Goals: Celebrate with fellow fans when the Lightning score a goal. The arena erupts with cheers and excitement, making every goal a memorable moment.

Attending a Tampa Bay Lightning hockey game is an unforgettable experience, whether you're a die-hard hockey fan or simply looking for an exciting night out in Tampa. The combination of thrilling on-ice action, a passionate fan base, and top-notch entertainment makes it a must-see event in the Tampa Bay area.

12. Take a scenic drive along Bayshore Boulevard.

Taking a scenic drive along Bayshore Boulevard in Tampa, Florida, is a delightful way to soak in breathtaking views, enjoy the waterfront, and experience the city's beauty. Here's what you can expect on your scenic drive along Bayshore Boulevard:

Stunning Waterfront Views: Bayshore Boulevard boasts one of the longest continuous sidewalk waterfronts in the world, offering unobstructed views of

Tampa Bay. The drive provides a picturesque backdrop of the bay, with sailboats, pelicans, and the city skyline in the distance.

Majestic Mansions: As you drive along Bayshore Boulevard, you'll pass by some of Tampa's most beautiful and historic mansions. These grand homes showcase a range of architectural styles and add charm to the scenic drive.

Fitness and Recreation: Bayshore Boulevard is a popular spot for fitness enthusiasts. You'll encounter joggers, cyclists, and walkers along the scenic path, making it a vibrant and active area.

Gasparilla Invasion: If you're visiting during the Gasparilla Pirate Festival, you can witness the pirate ship invasion along Bayshore Boulevard. It's a unique and lively event that celebrates Tampa's pirate heritage.

Photo Opportunities: The picturesque views, scenic greenery, and impressive homes make Bayshore Boulevard a fantastic location for taking photographs. Be sure to capture the beauty of the bay and the city.

Seating Areas: There are several parks and seating areas along the route, including Ballast Point Park and Bayshore Linear Park, where you can stop and enjoy a picnic or simply take in the views.

Historical Markers: Look for historical markers along the boulevard that provide insights into Tampa's history and its connection to the bay.

Sunsets: Bayshore Boulevard is known for its breathtaking sunsets. As the day draws to a close, you can witness the sun setting over Tampa Bay, creating a magical and romantic atmosphere.

Special Events: The boulevard occasionally hosts special events, parades, and community gatherings, so check the local event calendar to see if there are any festivities taking place during your visit.

Cafes and Restaurants: Bayshore Boulevard is lined with cafes and restaurants, making it easy to stop for a meal, coffee, or a refreshing drink while enjoying the views.

Relaxation: The leisurely pace of the drive allows you to relax, unwind, and escape the hustle and bustle of the city. It's an opportunity to connect with nature and enjoy the waterfront.

Bike Rentals: If you prefer cycling, consider renting a bike to explore Bayshore Boulevard at your own pace. There are bike rental options available in the area.

Community Feel: The drive along Bayshore Boulevard provides a sense of community and camaraderie, as locals and visitors come together to appreciate the natural beauty of Tampa Bay.

Whether you're visiting Tampa for the first time or you're a resident looking for a peaceful and scenic escape, a drive along Bayshore Boulevard offers a memorable and picturesque experience that showcases the city's charm and waterfront allure.

13. Visit the Tampa Museum of Art.

Visiting the Tampa Museum of Art is an enriching and culturally rewarding experience in the heart of Tampa, Florida. Here's what you can expect when you explore this notable museum:

Art Collections: The Tampa Museum of Art houses an impressive collection of art from various time periods and regions. You can expect to see a diverse range of artworks, including paintings, sculptures, decorative arts, and more.

Exhibition Galleries: The museum features rotating exhibitions that showcase both permanent collection pieces and temporary exhibitions from renowned artists and collections worldwide. These exhibitions offer fresh and engaging content for visitors.

Contemporary Art: The Tampa Museum of Art places a strong emphasis on contemporary art, making it a hub for modern artistic expression. You'll have the opportunity to discover innovative and thought-provoking works.

Educational Programs: The museum offers educational programs and workshops for visitors of all ages, including art classes, lectures, and guided tours. These programs help enhance your understanding and appreciation of art.

Interactive Exhibits: Some exhibitions feature interactive elements that allow you to engage with the artwork in unique and immersive ways. These hands-on experiences add depth to your visit.

Local Artists: In addition to showcasing international and national artists, the museum often highlights the works of talented local artists, providing a platform for the region's creative talent.

Architectural Beauty: The museum's building itself is a work of art. Designed by architect Stanley Saitowitz, the building's sleek and modern design is an architectural attraction in its own right.

Waterfront Location: The Tampa Museum of Art is located along the Hillsborough River, offering beautiful waterfront views. You can enjoy scenic walks along the riverfront before or after your museum visit.

Museum Store: Browse the museum store for art-related books, unique gifts, and souvenirs that allow you to take a piece of your visit home with you.

Cultural Events: The museum frequently hosts cultural events, including art openings, lectures, and film screenings. Check the museum's calendar for upcoming events during your visit.

Café and Dining: Some museum locations have on-site cafes or dining options, providing a convenient place to grab a meal or refreshments during your visit.

Accessibility: The museum is committed to ensuring accessibility for all visitors, including those with disabilities. It provides facilities and services to accommodate diverse needs.

Photography: While many museums have restrictions on photography, the Tampa Museum of Art often allows photography of its permanent collection, so you can capture memories of your favorite artworks.

Art Garden: Some locations include outdoor art installations and sculpture gardens, creating a serene and artistic outdoor space to explore.

Membership: Consider becoming a museum member to enjoy benefits such as free admission, exclusive access to events, and discounts at the museum store.

The Tampa Museum of Art is a cultural gem that offers a window into the world of art, creativity, and human expression. Whether you're an art enthusiast or simply looking to appreciate beauty and culture, a visit to this museum provides an enriching and inspiring experience.

14.Try Cuban coffee at a local cafe.

Trying Cuban coffee at a local cafe in Tampa is a flavorful and energizing experience that allows you to savor the rich and bold flavors of Cuban coffee culture. Here's what you can expect when you order Cuban coffee:

Cafecito: The most famous Cuban coffee preparation is the "cafecito" or "cafecito Cubano." It's a strong and sweet espresso shot that's typically served in a small cup, often with a side of a glass of water.

Flavorful Espresso: Cuban coffee is known for its intense and bold flavor. It's brewed with finely ground dark roast coffee beans, producing a robust and aromatic espresso.

Sweetness: What sets Cuban coffee apart is its sweetness. Traditional Cuban coffee is sweetened using sugar that is blended with the coffee grounds during brewing. This results in a distinct and sugary taste.

Cuban Colada: If you're sharing coffee with friends or colleagues, you might order a "Cuban colada," which is a larger portion of cafecito served in a small container with multiple cups for sharing.

Cortadito: Another popular Cuban coffee variation is the "cortadito," which is similar to the cafecito but cut with a small amount of steamed milk, creating a creamier texture.

Café con Leche: For a milder coffee experience, try a "café con leche," which is a Cuban coffee with a generous amount of warm milk. It's a comforting and rich drink, often served in a larger cup.

Local Cafes: Tampa has a thriving Cuban and Latin American culinary scene, so you'll find many local cafes and bakeries that serve authentic Cuban coffee. Look for establishments with Cuban flags or signs advertising Cuban coffee.

Cafeteria Windows: Some cafes in Tampa have "ventanitas" or cafeteria windows where you can order Cuban coffee to go. It's a traditional way of serving coffee in Cuban culture.

Pastry Pairing: Consider pairing your Cuban coffee with a delicious Cuban pastry, such as a "pastelito" (sweet pastry filled with guava, cheese, or meat) or a "croqueta" (croquette filled with ham or chicken).

Social Experience: Enjoying Cuban coffee is often a social experience. Many locals gather at cafes and ventanitas to chat, sip coffee, and savor pastries while catching up with friends and neighbors.

Sip Slowly: Cuban coffee is strong, so sipping it slowly allows you to fully appreciate its flavor and aroma. It can provide a quick pick-me-up or a leisurely coffee break, depending on your preference.

Coffee Ritual: Ordering and drinking Cuban coffee is a cherished ritual in Cuban and Latin American culture. Embrace the tradition and take your time to savor every sip.

Trying Cuban coffee in Tampa is a cultural and culinary adventure that introduces you to the bold flavors and warm hospitality of the city's Cuban community. Whether you're a coffee connoisseur or simply looking to experience a taste of Tampa's diverse culture, a cup of Cuban coffee is a must-try treat.

15.Explore the Tampa Bay Performing Arts Center.

Exploring the Straz Center for the Performing Arts (formerly known as the Tampa Bay Performing Arts Center) in Tampa, Florida, is a cultural journey that allows you to immerse yourself in the world of performing arts. Here's what you can expect when you visit this renowned venue:

Variety of Performances: The Straz Center hosts a wide range of performing arts events, including Broadway shows, musicals, ballet, opera, symphony concerts, dance performances, comedy acts, and more. Check the event schedule to see what's currently playing during your visit.

Multiple Theaters: The Straz Center boasts multiple theaters of varying sizes, each designed to create an intimate and immersive experience for the audience. These include the Carol Morsani Hall, the Ferguson Hall, the Jaeb Theater, and the TECO Theater.

Broadway Series: The center is known for its Broadway Series, which brings some of the most popular Broadway shows to Tampa. It's an opportunity to see award-winning productions and touring casts.

Local and National Talent: In addition to national and international acts, the Straz Center also showcases local talent through community theater productions, school performances, and partnerships with local arts organizations.

Educational Programs: The center is committed to arts education and offers a variety of educational programs for students, teachers, and the community. These programs include workshops, school field trips, and masterclasses.

Riverwalk Access: The Straz Center is conveniently located along the Tampa Riverwalk, allowing you to take a scenic stroll along the Hillsborough River before or after a performance. It's a picturesque setting for a leisurely walk.

Pre-Show Dining: Some performances at the Straz Center offer pre-show dining options at on-site restaurants, such as Maestro's Restaurant, where you can enjoy a meal before the show.

Art Exhibits: The center often features rotating art exhibits in its lobby areas, providing a visual treat for art enthusiasts.

Ticketing and Box Office: You can purchase tickets for performances at the Straz Center online, over the phone, or in person at the box office. It's advisable to book your tickets in advance, especially for popular shows.

Accessibility: The Straz Center is committed to accessibility and offers services for patrons with disabilities, including accessible seating and assistive listening devices.

Parking: There is parking available at the Straz Center, but it can get crowded, especially during sold-out performances. Consider arriving early to secure a parking spot or explore alternative transportation options.

Dress Code: While there isn't a strict dress code, many patrons choose to dress up for the occasion, especially for evening performances.

Cultural Hub: The Straz Center serves as a cultural hub for the Tampa Bay area, attracting artists and performers from around the world. It plays a vital role in the local arts scene and community.

Visiting the Straz Center for the Performing Arts offers an opportunity to appreciate the arts, be it through a dazzling Broadway show, a moving orchestral performance, or a thought-provoking play. It's a cultural destination that brings the magic of live theater and music to the heart of Tampa.

16.Go birdwatching at Lettuce Lake Regional Park.

Birdwatching at Lettuce Lake Regional Park in Tampa, Florida, is a rewarding outdoor activity that allows you to observe a diverse range of bird species in their natural habitat. Here's what you can expect when you go birdwatching at Lettuce Lake Regional Park:

Abundant Birdlife: Lettuce Lake Regional Park is home to a wide variety of bird species, making it a prime spot for birdwatching. Commonly spotted birds include herons, egrets, ibises, woodpeckers, ospreys, eagles, hawks, owls, and many more.

Scenic Wetlands: The park features lush wetlands, a hardwood forest, and a picturesque lake. These diverse ecosystems provide habitats for different bird species, attracting both migratory and resident birds.

Boardwalks and Trails: Explore the park's network of boardwalks and nature trails that wind through the wetlands and along the lake. These trails offer excellent vantage points for birdwatching and provide opportunities for up-close encounters with nature.

Observation Tower: Climb the park's observation tower for a panoramic view of the wetlands and lake. It's an ideal spot to spot birds from above and get a broader perspective of the park's natural beauty.

Wildlife Photography: Bring your camera or binoculars to capture stunning photographs of the birds and other wildlife you encounter. The park's scenic surroundings make for excellent photo opportunities.

Educational Signage: Look for informational signs and displays along the trails, which can help you identify the bird species you encounter and learn more about the park's ecology.

Alligator Watching: While birdwatching, keep an eye out for alligators, turtles, and other wildlife that inhabit the park's wetlands. Exercise caution and observe these animals from a safe distance.

Seasonal Migration: Depending on the time of year, you may witness seasonal bird migrations, which can bring a unique set of species to the area.

Binoculars and Field Guides: Consider bringing binoculars and field guides to aid in bird identification and to get a closer look at distant birds.

Quiet Observation: Birdwatching often requires patience and quiet observation. Move slowly and quietly to avoid startling the birds and disrupting their natural behavior.

Early Morning and Late Afternoon: Birds are most active during the early morning and late afternoon, so these times are generally the best for birdwatching.

Pack Essentials: Bring essentials like water, sunscreen, insect repellent, and comfortable walking shoes to ensure a comfortable and enjoyable birdwatching experience.

Respect Nature: Practice ethical birdwatching by not disturbing nests, maintaining a safe distance from wildlife, and following park rules and guidelines.

Lettuce Lake Regional Park is a peaceful oasis within the city of Tampa, offering birdwatchers and nature enthusiasts a chance to connect with Florida's diverse avian population while immersing themselves in the natural beauty of the wetlands and forests. It's an ideal destination for both novice and experienced birdwatchers to enjoy the serenity of the outdoors.

17. Visit the University of South Florida Botanical Gardens.

Visiting the University of South Florida Botanical Gardens is a delightful way to immerse yourself in the beauty of nature and explore a diverse range of plant species in a serene setting. Here's what you can expect when you visit these botanical gardens in Tampa, Florida:

Botanical Diversity: The University of South Florida Botanical Gardens is home to a wide variety of plant species from around the world. You can explore gardens featuring tropical, subtropical, desert, wetland, and native Florida plants.

Educational Experience: The gardens serve as an educational resource, providing information about plant species, their ecological importance, and their cultural significance. Interpretive signs and labels are often present to enhance your understanding.

Garden Themes: The gardens are organized into different themed areas, each showcasing a unique collection of plants. You can stroll through areas like the butterfly garden, bromeliad garden, palm garden, rose garden, and more.

Water Features: Many parts of the gardens feature tranquil water features, including ponds, fountains, and meandering streams, creating a soothing and picturesque ambiance.

Butterfly House: The butterfly garden includes a butterfly house where you can observe colorful butterflies up close and learn about their life cycles and behavior.

Seasonal Blooms: Depending on the time of year, you can experience seasonal blooms and the changing colors of various flowers, shrubs, and trees.

Birdwatching: The gardens are a haven for birdwatchers, with numerous bird species that visit or reside in the lush vegetation. Keep an eye out for resident and migratory birds.

Photography: Bring your camera to capture the vibrant colors, intricate textures, and natural beauty of the plants and gardens. It's a great location for photography enthusiasts.

Events and Workshops: The gardens often host special events, workshops, and educational programs related to horticulture, gardening, and conservation. Check their event calendar for upcoming activities.

Gift Shop: Many botanical gardens have gift shops where you can purchase souvenirs, books, and gardening-related items.

Relaxation: The gardens provide a peaceful atmosphere, making it an ideal place for a leisurely stroll, meditation, or a quiet escape from the hustle and bustle of daily life.

Picnicking: Some botanical gardens offer picnic areas where you can enjoy a meal amid the natural beauty. Consider bringing a picnic lunch to make the most of your visit.

Accessibility: The gardens are typically accessible to visitors of all abilities, with paved pathways and accommodations for wheelchairs and strollers.

Membership: If you plan to visit frequently, consider becoming a member of the botanical gardens to enjoy benefits such as free admission, discounts, and special access.

The University of South Florida Botanical Gardens provides a tranquil and educational experience where you can connect with the wonders of the plant kingdom. Whether you're a botany enthusiast, a nature lover, or simply seeking a peaceful outdoor escape, a visit to these gardens offers a refreshing and visually captivating journey.

18.Take a cruise on the StarShip Dining Yacht.

Taking a cruise on the StarShip Dining Yacht in Tampa, Florida, is a unique and luxurious experience that combines fine dining with scenic views of Tampa Bay. Here's what you can expect when you embark on a cruise aboard the StarShip:

Luxurious Vessel: The StarShip is a spacious and elegant yacht designed for comfort and style. It features multiple decks, including dining rooms, lounges, and outdoor observation areas, allowing you to choose your preferred setting.

Scenic Views: As you cruise along Tampa Bay, you'll be treated to stunning waterfront views, including the downtown Tampa skyline, waterfront mansions, and natural landscapes. The changing scenery provides a beautiful backdrop for your dining experience.

Gourmet Dining: The StarShip offers gourmet dining experiences with carefully crafted menus. Depending on the cruise package you choose, you can enjoy a multi-course meal, a buffet, or specialty cuisine prepared by skilled chefs.

Live Entertainment: Many StarShip cruises include live entertainment, such as music, dancing, and performances. The onboard entertainment enhances the atmosphere and creates a memorable experience.

Cocktail and Bar Service: The yacht typically has a full-service bar where you can order a variety of cocktails, wines, and beverages to complement your meal.

Special Occasions: The StarShip is a popular venue for special occasions, including weddings, anniversaries, birthdays, and corporate events. Consider booking a private event or a themed cruise for a memorable celebration.

Sunset Cruises: Sunset cruises are a popular choice, as they offer a romantic and picturesque setting as the sun dips below the horizon. It's an ideal option for couples looking for a memorable date night.

Narrated Tours: Some cruises offer narrated tours that provide historical and cultural insights into the Tampa Bay area. Learn about the region's history and landmarks as you cruise.

Photography Opportunities: The picturesque views and elegant yacht make for excellent photography opportunities. Capture the beauty of the bay and your memorable moments on board.

Professional Crew: The StarShip's crew is attentive and professional, ensuring that you have a comfortable and enjoyable experience throughout the cruise.

Dress Code: Depending on the cruise, there may be a dress code. Some cruises are more casual, while others have a more formal or themed attire requirement.

Reservations: It's advisable to make reservations in advance, especially for popular cruises and special events. Check the StarShip Dining Yacht's website for cruise schedules and availability.

A cruise on the StarShip Dining Yacht offers a combination of gourmet dining, entertainment, and scenic beauty that makes for a memorable and romantic experience in Tampa. Whether you're celebrating a special occasion or simply looking for an elegant night out, this unique dining cruise provides an unforgettable journey on the waters of Tampa Bay.

19.Explore the Henry B. Plant Museum at the University of Tampa.

Exploring the Henry B. Plant Museum at the University of Tampa is a fascinating journey into the Gilded Age history of Tampa and the legacy of Henry B. Plant, a prominent figure in the development of Florida. Here's what you can expect when you visit this museum:

Historic Setting: The museum is housed in the iconic Tampa Bay Hotel, which was built by Henry B. Plant in 1891. The hotel is a National Historic Landmark and an architectural gem, featuring Moorish and Victorian-inspired design elements.

Museum Exhibits: The Henry B. Plant Museum features a collection of exhibits that take you back in time to the late 19th century. Explore the rooms and corridors of the former hotel, which have been meticulously preserved and restored.

Gilded Age Decor: Admire the opulent interior with its rich Victorian furnishings, stained glass windows, and period decor. Learn about the lavish lifestyle of the elite who once stayed at the Tampa Bay Hotel.

Henry B. Plant's Legacy: Gain insights into the life and business ventures of Henry B. Plant, who played a pivotal role in developing Florida's transportation and tourism industries. His contributions to the region's growth are a central theme of the museum.

Tampa's History: The museum also provides a broader understanding of Tampa's history, from its early days as a small settlement to its emergence as a major transportation hub and tourist destination.

Educational Programs: The museum offers educational programs, lectures, and workshops that delve deeper into the history of the Tampa Bay Hotel, the Gilded Age, and Henry B. Plant's impact on the region.

Rotating Exhibits: In addition to its permanent collection, the museum often hosts temporary and rotating exhibits that explore different aspects of history and culture.

Gardens and Grounds: The museum's gardens and exterior are worth exploring. Take a leisurely stroll through the lush gardens surrounding the hotel, which offer a tranquil and scenic retreat.

Gift Shop: The museum has a gift shop where you can find unique souvenirs, books, and historic items related to Tampa and the Gilded Age.

Events: Check the museum's event calendar for special exhibitions, programs, and events that may be taking place during your visit.

Accessibility: The museum is committed to providing access to all visitors, including those with disabilities. It offers accessible facilities and services.

Tours: Guided tours of the museum are available, providing in-depth information and stories about the Tampa Bay Hotel and its history.

Visitor Center: Start your visit at the museum's visitor center, where you can get maps, information, and tickets for your tour.

Exploring the Henry B. Plant Museum offers a glimpse into the elegance and opulence of the Gilded Age, as well as the visionary efforts of Henry B. Plant in shaping the history of Tampa and Florida. It's an enriching and culturally significant experience for history enthusiasts and anyone interested in the region's heritage.

20.Go kayaking in Tampa's waterways.

Kayaking in Tampa's waterways is a fantastic way to explore the city's natural beauty, get some exercise, and enjoy the outdoors. Here's what you can expect when you go kayaking in Tampa:

Kayaking Locations: Tampa offers various kayaking opportunities in its rivers, bayous, estuaries, and coastal areas. Popular kayaking destinations include the Hillsborough River, the Alafia River, the Little Manatee River, the Tampa Bay coastline, and many more.

Kayak Rentals: If you don't have your own kayak, you can easily rent one from local outfitters and kayak rental companies. They typically provide kayaks, paddles, life vests, and sometimes guided tours.

Different Skill Levels: Tampa's waterways cater to kayakers of all skill levels, from beginners to experienced paddlers. Choose routes and water bodies that match your skill level and preferences.

Scenic Beauty: Kayaking allows you to immerse yourself in the natural beauty of Tampa. Paddle through mangrove tunnels, cypress-lined rivers, and estuaries teeming with wildlife. Keep an eye out for dolphins, manatees, birds, and other local fauna.

Sunset Kayaking: Sunset kayaking is a magical experience in Tampa. Paddle out onto the water in the late afternoon and watch the sun dip below the horizon, casting stunning colors across the sky and water.

Mangrove Tunnels: Some kayaking routes take you through intricate mangrove tunnels, providing a unique and serene experience as you navigate the winding waterways.

Eco-Tours: Consider joining an eco-tour guided by naturalists who can provide insights into the local ecology, wildlife, and conservation efforts.

Fishing: If you enjoy fishing, some kayaking spots in Tampa are excellent for angling. You can catch a variety of fish species in the region's waters.

Safety First: Always wear a life vest, stay hydrated, and follow safety guidelines while kayaking. Tampa's waterways can vary in current and conditions, so it's essential to prioritize safety.

Tidal Considerations: Be aware of tidal changes, especially if you're kayaking in coastal areas or estuaries. Tides can affect water levels and currents.

Packing Essentials: Bring essentials like sunscreen, a hat, sunglasses with a strap, water-resistant bags for personal items, and a whistle for safety.

Respect Nature: Practice responsible kayaking by respecting wildlife and the environment. Avoid disturbing nesting birds and wildlife, and follow Leave No Trace principles.

Group or Solo: You can kayak individually, with a partner, or as part of a guided group tour. Choose the option that suits your preferences and experience level.

Rent or Bring Your Kayak: Whether you rent a kayak or bring your own, kayaking in Tampa provides a memorable and immersive way to connect with nature and experience the region's unique waterways.

Kayaking in Tampa's waterways offers a peaceful and eco-friendly way to explore the city's natural wonders, observe wildlife, and enjoy the serenity of the outdoors. It's an activity that appeals to both nature enthusiasts and adventure seekers alike.

21.Attend a live concert at Amalie Arena.

Attending a live concert at Amalie Arena in Tampa, Florida, is an exhilarating experience that allows you to enjoy world-class music performances in a state-of-the-art venue. Here's what you can expect when you attend a concert at Amalie Arena:

World-Class Venue: Amalie Arena is one of Tampa's premier entertainment venues, known for its modern architecture, excellent acoustics, and top-notch facilities. It's the home of the Tampa Bay Lightning NHL team and hosts a wide range of events, including concerts.

Concert Lineup: The arena hosts concerts by a diverse array of artists and bands, from international superstars to up-and-coming acts. Check the arena's event calendar to see which artists are performing during your visit.

Seating Options: Amalie Arena offers various seating options, including floor seats close to the stage, lower-level and upper-level seats, suites, and club seating. Choose the seating category that suits your preferences and budget.

Sound and Visual Experience: The arena is designed to provide an exceptional audio and visual experience for concertgoers. State-of-the-art sound systems and large video screens ensure that you won't miss a moment of the performance.

Concession Stands: You'll find a variety of concession stands and dining options inside the arena, offering a range of food and beverages. Enjoy classic arena fare, snacks, and specialty items.

Merchandise: Many concerts feature merchandise stands where you can purchase artist merchandise, including T-shirts, posters, and memorabilia to commemorate the event.

Security Measures: Amalie Arena has security measures in place to ensure the safety of all attendees. Be prepared for bag checks and metal detectors when entering the venue.

Arrive Early: To secure the best parking and seating options, it's advisable to arrive early, especially for popular concerts. Consider using public transportation or ridesharing services to avoid parking hassles.

Tailgating: Some events may allow for pre-concert tailgating in designated areas. Check the event details for specific policies.

Accessible Facilities: The arena provides accessible seating and facilities for patrons with disabilities. If you require any accommodations, contact the venue in advance.

Atmosphere: The energy and excitement of a live concert at Amalie Arena are unparalleled. Be prepared to sing along, dance, and join the crowd in creating unforgettable memories.

Parking: Amalie Arena offers parking options in nearby lots and garages. Plan your parking in advance and consider using the arena's website or app to purchase parking passes.

Post-Show: After the concert, consider exploring the nearby downtown Tampa area, which offers a variety of restaurants, bars, and nightlife options to continue your evening.

Attending a live concert at Amalie Arena is an opportunity to immerse yourself in the music, connect with fellow fans, and enjoy a memorable night of entertainment in the heart of Tampa. Whether you're a dedicated fan of the artist or simply looking for a great night out, a concert at Amalie Arena is sure to be a thrilling experience.

22. Visit the Glazer Children's Museum.

Visiting the Glazer Children's Museum in Tampa, Florida, is a fun and educational experience for families and children of all ages. Here's what you can expect when you explore this interactive and engaging museum:

Hands-On Exhibits: The Glazer Children's Museum is filled with interactive and hands-on exhibits designed to inspire curiosity, creativity, and learning. Children can engage in activities that promote critical thinking and problem-solving.

Diverse Themes: The museum features a variety of themed areas and exhibits, such as science, art, technology, health, and more. Each section offers a different learning experience and encourages exploration.

Play and Imagination: Children are encouraged to use their imaginations and play in a safe and stimulating environment. From building structures to pretending to be scientists, there's something for every interest.

Learning Through Play: The museum's approach is grounded in the idea that children learn best through play. Through play-based activities, children can develop important cognitive and social skills.

Toddler Play Zone: There is often a designated area for younger children, including toddlers and preschoolers, where they can engage in age-appropriate activities and play.

Special Exhibitions: In addition to its permanent exhibits, the museum frequently hosts special exhibitions and events, so there's always something new to discover.

Outdoor Play: Some museum locations have outdoor play areas that provide an opportunity for children to get some fresh air and enjoy physical activities.

Educational Programs: The Glazer Children's Museum offers educational programs, workshops, and classes that are both entertaining and informative. Check their schedule for any upcoming events.

Birthday Parties: The museum is a popular venue for children's birthday parties. Consider hosting your child's special day here for a unique and engaging celebration.

Cafeteria: Some locations have on-site cafeterias or dining options where you can grab a meal or snack during your visit.

Membership: If you plan to visit the museum regularly, consider becoming a member. Membership often includes benefits like free admission, discounts, and exclusive access to special events.

Accessibility: The museum strives to be accessible to all children, including those with disabilities. It provides accommodations and resources to ensure that everyone can enjoy the exhibits.

Gift Shop: Browse the museum's gift shop for educational toys, books, and souvenirs that can extend the learning experience at home.

Visiting the Glazer Children's Museum is a fantastic way for children to engage their minds, explore their interests, and have a great time while learning. It's a place where families can bond, play, and create lasting memories together while nurturing a love for lifelong learning.

23.Explore the Tampa Bay Watch Discovery Center.

Exploring the Tampa Bay Watch Discovery Center is an opportunity to learn about the unique ecosystem of Tampa Bay and the importance of environmental conservation. Here's what you can expect when you visit this educational center in Tampa, Florida:

Educational Exhibits: The Tampa Bay Watch Discovery Center features a variety of exhibits that highlight the rich biodiversity of Tampa Bay. Learn about the bay's aquatic life, plant species, and the delicate balance of this coastal ecosystem.

Interactive Displays: Many exhibits are interactive, allowing visitors of all ages to engage with the content. Children and adults alike can enjoy hands-on learning experiences that make science and conservation fun.

Marine Life: Discover the marine life that calls Tampa Bay home, from fish and crabs to sea birds and dolphins. Gain insights into the habitats and behaviors of these creatures.

Coastal Habitats: Explore different coastal habitats found in the Tampa Bay area, including seagrass beds, mangrove forests, and oyster reefs. Learn how these ecosystems support the bay's health and sustainability.

Conservation Efforts: The Tampa Bay Watch Discovery Center provides information about the conservation initiatives and restoration projects carried out by Tampa Bay Watch, a nonprofit organization dedicated to protecting and restoring Tampa Bay.

Educational Programs: The center often hosts educational programs, workshops, and events focused on marine science, conservation, and environmental stewardship. Check their schedule for upcoming activities.

Guided Tours: Consider joining a guided tour of the center to get in-depth insights into Tampa Bay's ecology and conservation efforts. Knowledgeable guides can answer your questions and provide additional context.

Virtual Reality Experiences: Some centers incorporate virtual reality technology to give visitors a unique perspective on Tampa Bay's underwater world. These experiences can be both educational and entertaining.

Scenic Location: Enjoy scenic views of Tampa Bay from the Discovery Center's location. You may even spot wildlife in the surrounding natural areas.

Gift Shop: Browse the center's gift shop for eco-friendly merchandise, books, and souvenirs that support the organization's conservation efforts.

Family-Friendly: The center is designed to be family-friendly, making it an excellent destination for kids and parents to learn together.

Environmental Advocacy: Learn about ways you can get involved in local environmental conservation efforts and become an advocate for the protection of Tampa Bay.

Accessibility: The center is typically accessible to visitors of all abilities, with accommodations in place for those with disabilities.

Visiting the Tampa Bay Watch Discovery Center is not only a chance to gain a deeper understanding of the ecological significance of Tampa Bay but also an opportunity to appreciate the efforts being made to preserve and protect this vital coastal ecosystem. It's an educational and inspirational experience for nature enthusiasts and anyone interested in the environment.

24. Explore the historic Hyde Park Village shopping district.

Exploring the historic Hyde Park Village shopping district in Tampa, Florida, is a delightful experience that combines upscale shopping, dining, and a charming atmosphere. Here's what you can expect when you visit this historic and stylish shopping destination:

Historic Ambiance: Hyde Park Village is located in the heart of Tampa's historic Hyde Park neighborhood. The district features tree-lined streets, brick-paved walkways, and classic architecture, giving it a distinctive and charming ambiance.

Upscale Boutiques: The shopping district is home to a variety of upscale boutiques and shops, offering a range of fashion, accessories, home decor, and specialty items. You'll find both well-known brands and unique, locally owned stores.

Dining Options: Hyde Park Village boasts a diverse selection of dining establishments, from trendy cafes to fine dining restaurants. Whether you're in the mood for a casual meal, coffee, or a gourmet dinner, you'll find options to suit your tastes.

Art and Culture: Some boutiques and galleries in the area may showcase local art, providing an opportunity to explore the local creative scene.

Outdoor Seating: Many restaurants and cafes in Hyde Park Village offer outdoor seating, allowing you to enjoy your meal or coffee al fresco while soaking in the district's atmosphere.

Event Space: The village often hosts events and gatherings, including outdoor markets, art festivals, and live entertainment. Check their event calendar for any happenings during your visit.

Entertainment: Depending on the season, you may find live music, street performers, or other entertainment options that enhance your shopping and dining experience.

Green Spaces: Hyde Park Village includes attractive green spaces and sitting areas where you can relax and take a break during your exploration.

Pet-Friendly: The district is known for being pet-friendly, so feel free to bring your furry friend along while you shop and dine.

Parking: There is usually convenient parking available within or near Hyde Park Village, making it easy to access the shops and restaurants.

Local Services: In addition to retail and dining, you may find services such as salons, spas, and fitness studios within the village.

Seasonal Decor: Depending on the time of year, the district may be adorned with seasonal decorations and displays, creating a festive and inviting atmosphere.

Exploring Hyde Park Village provides a mix of shopping, dining, and cultural experiences within a historic and picturesque setting. Whether you're looking for unique fashion finds, a memorable dining experience, or simply a leisurely stroll through a charming neighborhood, Hyde Park Village offers a welcoming and stylish destination in the heart of Tampa.

25.Take a day trip to Honeymoon Island State Park.

Taking a day trip to Honeymoon Island State Park near Tampa, Florida, is a wonderful way to enjoy the natural beauty of Florida's Gulf Coast. Here's what you can expect when you visit this scenic and pristine island park:

Beautiful Beaches: Honeymoon Island State Park boasts some of the most stunning beaches in the Tampa Bay area. The soft, white sands and clear waters of the Gulf of Mexico provide an ideal setting for sunbathing, swimming, and beachcombing.

Shelling: The park is renowned for its excellent shelling opportunities. Collect seashells along the shore, including unique and colorful specimens like sand dollars and lightning whelks.

Nature Trails: Explore the park's nature trails that wind through a variety of coastal habitats, including pine forests, mangrove swamps, and salt marshes. These trails offer opportunities for birdwatching and wildlife observation.

Osprey Trail: The Osprey Trail is a popular 2.5-mile loop trail that takes you through some of the island's most beautiful natural areas. Keep an eye out for ospreys, eagles, and other birds of prey.

Picnicking: Honeymoon Island State Park provides picnic areas with tables and grills, making it a great spot for a beachside picnic with family or friends.

Travel to Tampa Florida

Wildlife Viewing: The park is home to a diverse range of wildlife, including gopher tortoises, raccoons, armadillos, and various bird species. You may also spot dolphins and manatees swimming offshore.

Nature Center: Visit the Rotary Centennial Nature Center, which offers educational exhibits about the park's natural history, wildlife, and conservation efforts.

Pet-Friendly: Honeymoon Island is pet-friendly, and you can bring your dog to the pet-friendly beach area, but dogs must be kept on a leash.

Café and Gift Shop: The café and gift shop near the beach pavilion offer refreshments, snacks, and souvenirs.

Beach Amenities: Restrooms, outdoor showers, and changing facilities are available near the beach for your convenience.

Ferry to Caladesi Island: From Honeymoon Island, you can take a ferry to neighboring Caladesi Island, another beautiful state park known for its natural beauty and unspoiled beaches.

Kayaking and Paddleboarding: Bring your own kayak or rent one to explore the calm waters around the island. Paddleboarding is also a popular activity in the area.

Sunsets: Don't miss the opportunity to watch the sunset over the Gulf of Mexico. The park's western-facing beaches provide a spectacular view.

Entrance Fees: Please note that there is an entrance fee to access Honeymoon Island State Park. The fee varies depending on the number of occupants in your vehicle.

Honeymoon Island State Park offers a serene and natural escape just a short drive from Tampa. Whether you're seeking a day of relaxation on the beach, a chance to connect with nature, or a picturesque spot for outdoor activities, this island park provides a peaceful and scenic retreat along Florida's Gulf Coast.

26.Experience the Gasparilla Pirate Festival.

The Gasparilla Pirate Festival is a beloved and annual event in Tampa, Florida, known for its swashbuckling fun and vibrant pirate-themed celebrations. Here's what you can expect when you experience the Gasparilla Pirate Festival:

Pirate Invasion: The Gasparilla Pirate Festival is centered around the mythical pirate invasion of Tampa Bay by the legendary pirate Jose Gaspar (Gasparilla). As the "invasion" begins, a fully rigged pirate ship, the Jose Gasparilla, sails into the bay with a crew of costumed pirates, cannons booming, and flags flying.

Parade: The highlight of the festival is the Gasparilla Parade of Pirates, one of the largest and most extravagant parades in the Southeastern United States. The parade features colorful floats, marching bands, pirate krewes, and elaborate costumes. Be prepared to catch beads and treasures thrown from the floats.

Pirate Krewes: Gasparilla involves various pirate krewes, each with its own unique theme, costumes, and personalities. These krewes participate in the festivities and add to the overall spectacle.

Street Festivities: In addition to the parade, there are street festivals and celebrations held in various parts of Tampa. These include live music, food vendors, arts and crafts, and entertainment for all ages.

Pirate-Themed Attire: Many festivalgoers dress in pirate-themed attire, so don't be surprised to see people of all ages wearing eye patches, tricorn hats, and pirate costumes.

Treasure Hunt: Some Gasparilla events include treasure hunts and games for children, adding to the family-friendly atmosphere.

Fireworks: The festival often concludes with a spectacular fireworks display over the bay, providing a grand finale to the day's festivities.

Music and Entertainment: Live music and entertainment stages feature a variety of performances, from local bands to national headliners.

Gasparilla Invasion Brunch: Some events include a Gasparilla Invasion Brunch, where attendees can enjoy a meal while watching the invasion of the Jose Gasparilla.

Historical and Cultural Significance: Gasparilla has a rich history dating back over a century, and it celebrates Tampa's heritage and cultural diversity. It's a time for locals and visitors to come together in the spirit of community and fun.

Boating and Water Activities: Many spectators view the parade from boats anchored in Tampa Bay, creating a unique and nautical perspective on the festivities.

Safety and Crowd Management: Due to the large crowds, it's essential to plan your visit carefully. Be aware of road closures, parking options, and public transportation if you're attending the festival.

Gasparilla Pirate Festival is a beloved tradition in Tampa, celebrating the city's connection to pirate lore in a lively and entertaining way. Whether you're a pirate enthusiast, a fan of lively parades, or simply looking for a memorable event in Tampa, Gasparilla offers a one-of-a-kind experience that brings the spirit of adventure to Florida's Gulf Coast.

27.Try stand-up paddleboarding in Tampa Bay.

Trying stand-up paddleboarding (SUP) in Tampa Bay is a fantastic way to enjoy the water and the scenic beauty of the bay while getting some exercise. Here's what you can expect when you try stand-up paddleboarding in Tampa Bay:

Paddleboard Rentals: You can typically rent paddleboards from local watersports rental companies, many of which are located along the Tampa Bay coastline. They'll provide you with all the necessary equipment, including a paddle and a board.

SUP Lessons: If you're new to stand-up paddleboarding, consider taking a lesson from a local instructor or rental shop. They can teach you the basics of balance, paddling techniques, and safety tips.

Scenic Views: Paddling on Tampa Bay offers stunning views of the bay's calm waters, the downtown Tampa skyline, and the natural beauty of the surrounding areas. It's a great way to see the city from a unique perspective.

Caladesi Island and Honeymoon Island: You can paddle out to nearby Caladesi Island and Honeymoon Island State Parks, both of which offer pristine beaches, nature trails, and excellent opportunities for wildlife viewing.

Dolphin and Manatee Sightings: Tampa Bay is home to a variety of marine life, including dolphins and manatees. While stand-up paddleboarding, you might be lucky enough to spot these gentle creatures swimming nearby.

Fitness and Relaxation: SUP provides a full-body workout, engaging your core muscles as you balance and paddle. It's also a peaceful and meditative activity, allowing you to relax and enjoy the tranquility of the water.

Safety Considerations: Always wear a personal flotation device (PFD) while paddleboarding, especially if you're not a strong swimmer. Be mindful of weather conditions, tides, and currents, and check with local experts for safety advice.

Group and Guided Tours: Some rental shops offer guided paddleboard tours, which can be a great way to explore the bay with experienced guides who can point out interesting sights and share local knowledge.

Sun Protection: Don't forget to wear sunscreen, a hat, and sunglasses to protect yourself from the sun's rays. Consider bringing a water bottle to stay hydrated.

Respect Nature: When paddleboarding, be respectful of the environment. Avoid disturbing wildlife, especially nesting birds and sensitive coastal areas.

Photography Opportunities: Paddleboarding offers excellent photo opportunities. Capture the beauty of Tampa Bay, wildlife sightings, and your own memorable moments on the water.

Stand-up paddleboarding in Tampa Bay provides a peaceful and active way to connect with nature and enjoy the outdoors. Whether you're a beginner or an experienced paddler, it's an enjoyable activity that allows you to soak in the natural beauty of the bay and stay active while doing so.

28. Visit the Lowry Park Zoo.

Visiting the Lowry Park Zoo, now known as ZooTampa at Lowry Park, is a fantastic way to explore a diverse array of wildlife and enjoy family-friendly attractions in Tampa, Florida. Here's what you can expect when you visit this popular zoo:

Animal Exhibits: ZooTampa is home to a wide variety of animal species from around the world. Explore diverse exhibits showcasing animals like elephants, giraffes, big cats, primates, reptiles, manatees, and many more.

Conservation Efforts: The zoo is actively involved in conservation initiatives and provides educational information about its efforts to protect endangered species and preserve natural habitats.

Interactive Exhibits: Some animal exhibits feature interactive elements, allowing visitors to get up close and personal with certain animals. These hands-on experiences can be particularly enjoyable for children.

Manatee Rehabilitation Center: ZooTampa is known for its Manatee Critical Care Center, where injured or orphaned manatees are rehabilitated and prepared for release back into the wild.

Educational Programs: The zoo offers educational programs, animal encounters, and wildlife shows that provide insights into the behavior, biology, and conservation of various species. Check the schedule for daily activities.

Family-Friendly Attractions: In addition to animal exhibits, the zoo has family-friendly attractions, including a carousel, water play areas, and a children's zoo designed for younger visitors.

Safari Rides: Some areas of the zoo offer safari-style rides that provide a unique perspective on the animals' habitats. These rides often include guided commentary.

Botanical Gardens: Enjoy the lush botanical gardens throughout the zoo, featuring beautiful landscaping and exotic plants. It's a pleasant backdrop for your visit.

Dining Options: ZooTampa offers dining options ranging from casual to full-service restaurants and snack stands, allowing you to refuel during your visit.

Gift Shops: Browse the gift shops for animal-themed souvenirs, toys, clothing, and conservation-related merchandise.

Accessibility: The zoo is committed to being accessible to all visitors, including those with disabilities. Accessible pathways and facilities are available.

Special Events: Throughout the year, the zoo hosts special events like Boo at the Zoo (Halloween), Creatures of the Night (Halloween-themed event), and Wild Wonderland (holiday lights display).

Membership: Consider becoming a member if you plan to visit the zoo multiple times. Membership often includes benefits such as unlimited admission, discounts, and early access to special events.

Hours and Admission: Be sure to check the zoo's website for current hours of operation, admission prices, and any special requirements or policies.

Visiting ZooTampa at Lowry Park is an opportunity to connect with wildlife, learn about conservation, and enjoy a day of family-friendly fun. It's a great place for people of all ages to appreciate the wonders of the animal kingdom and the importance of protecting our natural world.

29.Explore the Tampa Theatre.

Exploring the Tampa Theatre is a journey into the rich history and elegant architecture of this historic landmark in Tampa, Florida. Here's what you can expect when you visit this beautifully restored movie palace:

Historic Architecture: Tampa Theatre is renowned for its stunning Mediterranean Revival architecture, featuring ornate details, opulent decor, and a starlit ceiling that mimics a night sky. The theater's design is a testament to the grand movie palaces of the 1920s.

Guided Tours: Consider taking a guided tour to learn about the theater's history, architectural significance, and behind-the-scenes details. Knowledgeable guides share fascinating stories and insights during these tours.

Classic Films: Tampa Theatre screens classic and independent films, offering a unique cinematic experience in a historic setting. Check the theater's schedule for screenings of beloved classics and new releases.

Travel to Tampa Florida

Live Performances: In addition to films, the theater hosts live performances, including concerts, comedy shows, and special events. It serves as a cultural hub for the Tampa Bay area.

Silent Film Series: Experience the magic of silent cinema with the theater's silent film series, often accompanied by live musical accompaniment, creating a nostalgic and immersive experience.

Special Events: Tampa Theatre hosts a variety of special events throughout the year, including film festivals, fundraisers, and community gatherings.

Art Exhibitions: The theater occasionally features art exhibitions in its lobby, showcasing the work of local artists.

Mighty Wurlitzer Organ: Tampa Theatre is home to a Mighty Wurlitzer organ, which is played before select screenings and events. The organ's music adds to the theater's vintage charm.

Concessions: Enjoy classic movie theater concessions like popcorn, candy, and soft drinks, as well as craft beer and wine, which are often available for purchase.

Private Events: Tampa Theatre is available for private events, including weddings, corporate gatherings, and private film screenings. Its unique ambiance adds a touch of elegance to any occasion.

Annual WineFest: The theater hosts an annual WineFest, featuring wine tastings, food pairings, and social events, with proceeds supporting the preservation of the historic theater.

Membership: Consider becoming a member of Tampa Theatre to enjoy benefits such as discounted tickets, advance ticket sales, and invitations to members-only events.

Accessibility: The theater is dedicated to providing accessibility for all patrons, including those with disabilities. Accessible seating and assistive listening devices are available.

Visiting Tampa Theatre is a step back in time to the golden age of cinema, where you can appreciate the artistry of film and the architectural beauty of a bygone era. Whether you're a movie enthusiast, a history buff, or someone looking for a unique entertainment experience, Tampa Theatre offers a cultural gem in the heart of Tampa's downtown district.

30.Go snorkeling in the Gulf of Mexico.

Snorkeling in the Gulf of Mexico is a fantastic way to explore the underwater world and discover the marine life of this beautiful region. Here's what you can expect when you go snorkeling in the Gulf of Mexico:

Warm Waters: The Gulf of Mexico offers relatively warm waters, especially during the spring and summer months, making it a comfortable environment for snorkeling.

Clear Visibility: Depending on the location and weather conditions, the Gulf of Mexico can provide clear water with good visibility, allowing you to see the marine life and underwater landscapes.

Marine Life: While snorkeling in the Gulf, you may encounter a variety of marine species, including fish, sea turtles, rays, dolphins, and a diverse range of colorful corals and sponges.

Reef Systems: Some areas of the Gulf are home to artificial and natural reef systems, which attract a multitude of marine creatures. These reefs offer excellent snorkeling opportunities.

Snorkeling Tours: Consider joining a snorkeling tour with experienced guides who can take you to the best snorkeling spots, provide safety instructions, and point out interesting marine life.

Equipment Rental: If you don't have your own snorkeling gear, many local outfitters and tour operators offer equipment rentals, including masks, snorkels, fins, and life jackets.

Safety First: Always prioritize safety when snorkeling. Be aware of currents, tides, and weather conditions. Snorkel with a buddy, stay within your comfort zone, and follow any safety guidelines provided by tour operators.

Environmental Responsibility: Be a responsible snorkeler by respecting the marine environment. Avoid touching or disturbing marine life, corals, and the seabed. Pack out any trash and avoid using sunscreen that may harm coral reefs.

Snorkeling Locations: Popular snorkeling spots in the Gulf of Mexico include destinations along the Florida coast, such as the Florida Keys, the Emerald Coast, and the Sarasota area. Each offers unique underwater experiences.

Dolphin Encounters: Some snorkeling tours in the Gulf may offer the chance to swim and interact with wild dolphins in their natural habitat. This is a thrilling experience but should be done with ethical and responsible operators.

Photography and Videography: Consider bringing an underwater camera or GoPro to capture the beauty of the underwater world and create lasting memories of your snorkeling adventure.

Boat and Shore Snorkeling: Depending on your preference and location, you can choose between boat-based snorkeling trips or snorkeling from the shore. Both options offer exciting opportunities to explore.

Snorkeling in the Gulf of Mexico is an opportunity to connect with the sea and witness the vibrant marine life that inhabits these waters. Whether you're an experienced snorkeler or a beginner, the Gulf offers diverse and captivating underwater experiences for nature enthusiasts and adventure seekers alike.

31.Attend a Tampa Bay Rays baseball game.

Attending a Tampa Bay Rays baseball game is a thrilling experience for sports enthusiasts and fans of America's favorite pastime. Here's what you can expect when you attend a game at Tropicana Field, the Rays' home stadium in St. Petersburg, Florida:

Game Schedule: Check the Tampa Bay Rays' official website or a reliable sports schedule for information on upcoming games, including dates, opponents, and game times.

Tickets: Purchase your tickets in advance through the team's official website, at the stadium's box office, or from authorized ticket vendors. Prices may vary depending on the seating section and the popularity of the game.

Seating Options: Tropicana Field offers a variety of seating options, from traditional stadium seats to luxury suites and premium club areas. Choose a seating category that suits your preferences and budget.

Gameday Atmosphere: Experience the excitement of a baseball game with the sounds of cheering fans, music, and the crack of the bat. Engage in the energy of the crowd as you root for the home team.

Concessions: Tropicana Field features a range of dining options, from classic ballpark fare like hot dogs and peanuts to more diverse and gourmet choices. Enjoy local and international flavors while watching the game.

Family-Friendly Activities: The stadium often provides family-friendly activities and attractions, such as a kids' play area, interactive games, and photo opportunities with team mascots.

Promotional Events: Keep an eye out for special promotional events, giveaways, and theme nights that may be scheduled for specific games.

Team Merchandise: Visit the team store to shop for Tampa Bay Rays merchandise, including jerseys, caps, and memorabilia to support your favorite players.

Entertainment: Between innings, enjoy entertainment on the stadium's video screens, including games, contests, and fan interactions.

Accessibility: Tropicana Field is designed to be accessible to all fans, including those with disabilities. Accessible seating and facilities are available.

Parking: Plan your parking in advance, as the stadium offers various parking options, including nearby lots and garages.

Rays Tank: One unique feature of Tropicana Field is the Rays Tank, a 10,000-gallon tank filled with rays and other marine life. It's a fascinating sight and a hit with fans.

Post-Game: After the game, consider exploring the surrounding area in St. Petersburg, which offers a variety of dining, entertainment, and cultural attractions.

Team History: Learn about the Tampa Bay Rays' history, achievements, and memorable moments through the team's displays and exhibits within the stadium.

Attending a Tampa Bay Rays baseball game is a great way to enjoy a day or evening of sports, entertainment, and camaraderie with fellow fans. Whether you're a die-hard baseball enthusiast or just looking for a fun outing, the experience of watching a live game at Tropicana Field is sure to be memorable.

32.Take a scenic sunset cruise.

Taking a scenic sunset cruise in Tampa Bay is a romantic and picturesque way to enjoy the stunning coastal views and the beauty of the setting sun. Here's what you can expect when you embark on a sunset cruise in Tampa Bay:

Breathtaking Sunsets: Tampa Bay is known for its spectacular sunsets, and a sunset cruise is the perfect way to witness nature's colorful display as the sun dips below the horizon.

Cruise Options: Several local operators offer a variety of sunset cruise options, from large sailboats to smaller, more intimate vessels. You can choose a cruise that matches your preferences, whether it's a romantic dinner cruise or a family-friendly excursion.

Scenic Waterways: Enjoy a leisurely cruise through Tampa Bay's scenic waterways, which may include views of the city skyline, waterfront mansions, wildlife habitats, and picturesque coastal landscapes.

Dolphin and Wildlife Sightings: Keep an eye out for playful dolphins and other marine life that often make appearances during sunset cruises. Birdwatchers may spot various seabird species.

Narration: Many cruise operators provide informative commentary about the area's history, wildlife, and natural landmarks, enhancing your understanding of the region.

Live Entertainment: Some cruises offer live entertainment, such as live music or onboard DJs, to create a lively and enjoyable atmosphere.

Dining Options: Depending on the cruise you choose, you may have access to onboard dining, including dinners, snacks, and beverages. Romantic sunset dinner cruises often feature gourmet meals.

BYOB Cruises: Some operators allow you to bring your own beverages, making it a personalized and budget-friendly option for enjoying a drink while watching the sunset.

Photography Opportunities: Be sure to bring your camera or smartphone to capture the stunning sunset and the beautiful surroundings. The changing colors and reflections on the water make for fantastic photo opportunities.

Private Charters: For a more exclusive experience, consider booking a private sunset charter for a special occasion like a proposal, anniversary, or birthday celebration.

Comfortable Seating: Sunset cruises typically provide comfortable seating, including outdoor decks and indoor cabins, ensuring a pleasant experience for all passengers.

Reservations: It's advisable to make reservations in advance, especially during peak tourist seasons, to secure your spot on the cruise of your choice.

Weather Considerations: Keep in mind that weather conditions can affect sunset cruises. Operators prioritize safety, so be prepared for possible rescheduling in the event of inclement weather.

Duration: Sunset cruises usually last around two hours, giving you plenty of time to enjoy the sights and the sunset.

A sunset cruise in Tampa Bay is a memorable and romantic experience, whether you're celebrating a special occasion or simply want to relax and soak in the natural beauty of the area. As you watch the sun paint the sky with vibrant colors, you'll create lasting memories of your time on the water.

33. Visit Big Cat Rescue.

Big Cat Rescue is a renowned sanctuary located in Tampa, Florida, dedicated to the rescue and rehabilitation of big cats, such as lions, tigers, leopards, and more. When you visit Big Cat Rescue, you can expect a unique and educational experience focused on conservation and animal welfare. Here's what you can expect during your visit:

Travel to Tampa Florida

Guided Tours: Big Cat Rescue offers guided tours led by knowledgeable and passionate staff and volunteers. These tours provide in-depth information about the sanctuary's mission, the history of the rescued cats, and the challenges facing big cats in captivity and in the wild.

Rescued Big Cats: Get up close to see the rescued big cats in their enclosures. Learn about each cat's individual story, their backgrounds, and the reasons they were brought to the sanctuary. You'll have the opportunity to observe these majestic animals in a safe and ethical environment.

Educational Programs: The sanctuary places a strong emphasis on education. You'll gain insights into the issues surrounding the big cat trade, including private ownership, roadside zoos, and the importance of protecting these animals and their habitats in the wild.

Conservation Initiatives: Discover the sanctuary's efforts to raise awareness about the conservation of big cats in the wild. You'll learn about the various species of big cats and the challenges they face in their native habitats.

Animal Welfare: Big Cat Rescue advocates for improved animal welfare standards and works to end the private ownership of big cats. You'll gain a deeper understanding of the ethical and humane treatment of these animals.

Photography Opportunities: Capture memorable photos of the big cats during your tour, as well as the sanctuary's beautiful surroundings and lush landscapes.

Gift Shop: Visit the sanctuary's gift shop to support their conservation efforts by purchasing souvenirs, apparel, and other items related to big cats and wildlife conservation.

Donations and Sponsorship: Consider making a donation or sponsoring a big cat to contribute to the care, well-being, and rescue efforts of these magnificent animals.

Guidelines and Safety: Follow the sanctuary's guidelines and safety instructions to ensure a respectful and safe visit for both visitors and the animals.

Booking in Advance: Due to the popularity of Big Cat Rescue, it's advisable to book your tour in advance, especially during peak visitor seasons.

Visiting Big Cat Rescue offers a unique opportunity to connect with these incredible creatures, while also supporting the sanctuary's vital mission of protecting big cats and raising awareness about the challenges they face. It's a chance to be inspired by the dedication of those working to make a positive difference in the lives of these magnificent animals.

34. Try jet skiing on the bay.

Jet skiing on the waters of Tampa Bay is an exhilarating and adventurous way to experience the beauty of the bay and enjoy some adrenaline-pumping fun. Here's what you can expect when you try jet skiing on Tampa Bay:

Rental Options: There are several water sports rental companies and marinas in the Tampa Bay area that offer jet ski rentals. You can typically rent a jet ski for a specified duration, such as an hour or half a day.

Safety Briefing: Before you set off on your jet ski adventure, the rental company will provide a safety briefing and instructions on how to operate the jet ski. Safety is a top priority, and life jackets are typically provided.

Exploration: Jet skiing on Tampa Bay allows you to explore the bay's vast expanse, including its calm waters, mangrove islands, and scenic shoreline. You can venture out on your own or follow guided tours.

Scenic Views: While jet skiing, you'll have the opportunity to take in the beautiful views of Tampa Bay, which may include glimpses of the city skyline, bridges, and coastal wildlife.

Adrenaline Rush: Jet skiing offers an adrenaline rush as you glide across the water at high speeds. Feel the wind in your hair and the spray of saltwater as you navigate the bay.

Wildlife Encounters: Keep an eye out for marine life such as dolphins, manatees, and various seabird species. Tampa Bay is home to diverse wildlife, and you may have the chance to see them in their natural habitat.

Photography: Bring a waterproof camera or a GoPro to capture the excitement of your jet skiing adventure and the scenic beauty of the bay.

Exploration Options: Depending on your experience level and the rental company, you can choose from guided tours, group jet ski outings, or solo adventures.

Equipment: Rental companies typically provide all the necessary equipment, including the jet ski, life jacket, and sometimes a wetsuit or rash guard.

Age and Licensing: Age restrictions and licensing requirements for jet skiing may vary depending on local regulations and rental policies. Ensure that you meet any age and licensing requirements before booking your jet ski rental.

Booking in Advance: Especially during peak tourist seasons, it's a good idea to book your jet ski rental in advance to secure your preferred date and time.

Jet skiing on Tampa Bay combines the thrill of water sports with the opportunity to explore the natural beauty of the bay. It's a memorable way to spend time outdoors, whether you're seeking adventure, relaxation, or a unique perspective on the coastal environment.

35.Explore the Manatee Viewing Center.

Exploring the Manatee Viewing Center near Tampa, Florida, is a wonderful way to observe these gentle giants in their natural habitat and learn about the local ecology. Here's what you can expect when you visit the Manatee Viewing Center:

Manatee Viewing: The primary attraction of the Manatee Viewing Center is, of course, the manatees. These large, slow-moving mammals are often seen in the warm waters of the adjacent Tampa Electric power plant's discharge canal during the winter months. Manatees gather here to seek refuge from the cold Gulf of Mexico waters.

Educational Exhibits: The center features educational exhibits and displays about manatees, their natural history, and the conservation efforts in place to protect them. You can learn about the manatee's habitat, diet, behavior, and the challenges they face in the wild.

Observation Platforms: The center provides elevated observation platforms and walkways that offer excellent vantage points for watching manatees and other wildlife. Binoculars are often available for visitors to use.

Mangrove Trail: Explore the center's mangrove trail, which winds through a beautiful coastal habitat. It's an opportunity to see various bird species, crabs, and other marine life in their natural environment.

Butterfly Garden: The center features a butterfly garden that attracts a variety of butterfly species. It's a peaceful spot to enjoy the beauty of nature.

Picnic Areas: Bring a picnic lunch and enjoy it in the designated picnic areas, complete with tables and scenic views.

Gift Shop: Visit the gift shop to purchase souvenirs, educational materials, and manatee-themed merchandise. Proceeds often support the center's conservation efforts.

Educational Programs: Check the center's schedule for educational programs, presentations, and ranger-led talks that offer insights into the local ecology and manatee conservation.

Photography: Bring your camera to capture memorable moments of manatee sightings and the surrounding natural beauty. Manatees often come close to the viewing areas, making for great photo opportunities.

Accessibility: The Manatee Viewing Center is typically accessible to all visitors, including those with disabilities. Accessible pathways and facilities are available.

Free Admission: In many cases, admission to the Manatee Viewing Center is free, making it an affordable and family-friendly attraction.

Seasonal Visits: Keep in mind that the best time to visit for manatee sightings is during the winter months when the Gulf waters are cooler.

The Manatee Viewing Center provides a unique opportunity to connect with nature and witness these gentle giants up close. It's a place where education, conservation, and the enjoyment of the natural world come together, offering a rewarding and memorable experience for visitors of all ages.

36.Go on a wildlife safari.

Embarking on a wildlife safari near Tampa, Florida, allows you to explore the region's natural beauty and observe a diverse range of wildlife species in their natural habitats. Here's what you can expect when you go on a wildlife safari in the Tampa Bay area:

Choice of Wildlife Areas: The Tampa Bay area offers various wildlife sanctuaries, parks, and natural preserves where you can go on a safari. Some popular options include Myakka River State Park, Circle B Bar Reserve, and the Chassahowitzka Wildlife Management Area.

Professional Guides: Many wildlife safari tours are led by experienced and knowledgeable guides who are well-versed in the local flora and fauna. They provide insights about the wildlife you encounter and the ecosystems you explore.

Diverse Wildlife: Depending on the location and season, you may have the chance to observe a wide range of wildlife, including alligators, birds (such as herons, egrets, and bald eagles), deer, wild hogs, otters, and various reptiles.

Scenic Landscapes: Wildlife safari tours often take you through beautiful natural landscapes, including wetlands, forests, and open grasslands. The scenery provides excellent photo opportunities.

Off-Road Adventures: Some safaris involve off-road experiences, where you'll travel in specialized vehicles or boats to access remote wildlife habitats that are not easily reachable by foot.

Binoculars and Equipment: Many safari operators provide binoculars and other equipment to enhance your wildlife viewing experience. Be sure to inquire about the amenities offered on your chosen tour.

Photography: Bring your camera or smartphone to capture the wildlife and scenic vistas. Be respectful of the animals and maintain a safe distance while photographing them.

Safety Measures: Wildlife safari tours prioritize safety for both participants and the animals. Guides will provide safety guidelines and instructions to ensure a responsible and enjoyable experience.

Timing: Wildlife sightings can vary depending on the time of day and season. Early morning and late afternoon tours are often recommended for the best chances of observing active wildlife.

Educational Opportunities: Learn about the local ecosystems, the behaviors of the animals you encounter, and the importance of conservation efforts to protect these natural habitats.

Weather Considerations: Be prepared for various weather conditions, as Florida can experience heat, rain, and humidity. Dress appropriately and bring sunscreen, insect repellent, and drinking water.

Duration: Safari tours can vary in duration, ranging from a few hours to a full day. Choose a tour that suits your interests and schedule.

A wildlife safari near Tampa is an exciting and educational adventure that allows you to appreciate the natural wonders of Florida's ecosystems. Whether you're a nature enthusiast, a birdwatcher, or simply looking to connect with the outdoors, a safari in the Tampa Bay area offers a chance to observe and learn about the diverse wildlife that calls this region home.

37.Visit the Salvador Dali Museum in nearby St. Petersburg.

Visiting the Salvador Dali Museum in nearby St. Petersburg, Florida, is a captivating and artistic experience that allows you to explore the life and works of one of the most renowned Surrealist artists of the 20th century. Here's what you can expect when you visit the Salvador Dali Museum:

World-Class Art Collection: The museum houses one of the most extensive collections of Salvador Dali's artworks outside of Europe. You'll have the opportunity to view a wide range of his paintings, drawings, sculptures, and other artistic creations.

Dali's Masterpieces: Marvel at some of Dali's most famous masterpieces, including "The Persistence of Memory," which features the iconic melting clocks, as well as "Christ of Saint John of the Cross" and "Gala Contemplating the Mediterranean Sea."

Architectural Beauty: The museum building itself is a work of art. Designed by architect Yann Weymouth, the structure is a stunning example of modern architecture and features a geodesic glass bubble known as the "enigma." It's a beautiful and unique setting for Dali's works.

Travel to Tampa Florida

Guided Tours: Consider taking a guided tour to gain deeper insights into Dali's life, artistic techniques, and the symbolism behind his works. Knowledgeable guides provide fascinating commentary during these tours.

Temporary Exhibitions: In addition to its permanent collection, the museum often hosts temporary exhibitions that explore various aspects of Dali's career, influences, and collaborations.

Educational Programs: The museum offers educational programs and workshops for all ages, making it an engaging destination for families, students, and art enthusiasts.

Dali Garden: Outside the museum, you'll find a tranquil garden featuring sculptures and greenery, providing a peaceful space to relax and reflect.

Gift Shop: Explore the museum's gift shop, which offers a wide selection of Dali-themed merchandise, books, and artwork for purchase.

Photography: Photography is allowed in most areas of the museum, so you can capture your favorite Dali works and share your experience with others.

Accessibility: The museum is committed to accessibility, with ramps, elevators, and accommodations for visitors with disabilities.

Dining Options: Nearby cafes and restaurants offer opportunities to enjoy a meal or refreshments before or after your museum visit.

Hours and Admission: Be sure to check the museum's website for current hours of operation, admission prices, and any special exhibitions or events.

Visiting the Salvador Dali Museum in St. Petersburg is a chance to immerse yourself in the surreal and imaginative world of one of the most influential artists of the 20th century. Whether you're a dedicated art lover or simply curious to explore Dali's eccentric and groundbreaking creations, the museum offers a thought-provoking and visually stunning experience.

38.Attend a Tampa Bay Rowdies soccer game.

Attending a Tampa Bay Rowdies soccer game is an exciting way to immerse yourself in the world of professional soccer and support one of Tampa's beloved sports teams. Here's what you can expect when you attend a Tampa Bay Rowdies game:

Game Schedule: Check the Tampa Bay Rowdies' official website or a sports schedule for information on upcoming games, including dates, opponents, and game times.

Tickets: Purchase your tickets in advance through the team's official website, at the stadium's box office, or from authorized ticket vendors. Ticket prices may vary depending on seating preferences and the importance of the match.

Stadium Atmosphere: The Rowdies play their home games at Al Lang Stadium, which offers an electric and passionate atmosphere during matches. You'll join fellow fans in cheering for the team.

Team Spirit: Get into the team spirit by wearing the Rowdies' colors and merchandise, including scarves, jerseys, and hats. The Rowdies have a dedicated and enthusiastic fan base.

Game Experience: Enjoy the thrill of live soccer as you watch the Rowdies take on their opponents. Feel the excitement as the team scores goals, makes impressive plays, and strives for victory.

Halftime Entertainment: Halftime often features entertaining activities, such as youth soccer exhibitions, contests, or performances, adding to the fun and energy of the game.

Concessions: Savor classic stadium fare, including hot dogs, popcorn, and soft drinks, while watching the match. Some stadiums also offer a selection of craft beers and local cuisine.

Family-Friendly Atmosphere: Rowdies games are family-friendly, and the team often provides activities for kids, making it an enjoyable outing for all ages.

Merchandise: Visit the team store to shop for Tampa Bay Rowdies merchandise, including apparel, scarves, and memorabilia to show your support.

Tailgating: Some fans engage in tailgating before games, creating a lively pre-game atmosphere with food, drinks, and camaraderie in the stadium's parking lots.

Accessibility: Al Lang Stadium is designed to be accessible to all fans, including those with disabilities. Accessible seating and facilities are available.

Post-Game: After the game, you can explore the vibrant downtown St. Petersburg area, which offers a variety of dining, entertainment, and cultural attractions.

Annual Events: Keep an eye out for special events, theme nights, and promotions that the Rowdies may host throughout the season.

Attending a Tampa Bay Rowdies soccer game is a thrilling experience that allows you to be part of the action and support your local team. Whether you're a dedicated soccer fan or looking for an exciting sports outing, you'll enjoy the dynamic atmosphere and camaraderie among fans as you cheer on the Rowdies.

39.Go on a ghost tour of Ybor City.

Exploring the haunted history of Ybor City through a ghost tour is a spine-tingling and fascinating way to learn about the area's past and the paranormal legends that have arisen over the years. Here's what you can expect when you go on a ghost tour of Ybor City:

Experienced Guides: Ghost tours are typically led by knowledgeable and entertaining guides who are well-versed in the history, folklore, and ghost stories of Ybor City. They'll share chilling tales and intriguing anecdotes about the area's haunted sites.

Haunted Locations: You'll visit some of Ybor City's most haunted locations, including historic buildings, streets, and landmarks that are said to be inhabited by restless spirits. These sites may have connections to the area's cigar industry, prohibition era, and immigrant history.

Ghosts and Legends: Learn about the ghostly apparitions, legends, and eerie occurrences associated with Ybor City's past. Stories may include tales of lost loves, tragic accidents, and mysterious events.

Historical Insights: Ghost tours often blend history and storytelling, providing insights into the rich and diverse history of Ybor City, from its origins as a cigar manufacturing hub to its cultural heritage.

Nighttime Atmosphere: Ghost tours typically take place in the evening or at night, creating an atmospheric and eerie ambiance that enhances the storytelling experience.

Walking Tours: Most Ybor City ghost tours are walking tours, allowing you to explore the haunted sites on foot and immerse yourself in the city's history. Wear comfortable shoes and be prepared to walk.

Photography: Bring your camera or smartphone to capture the haunted locations and the atmospheric surroundings. Some tours may even capture ghostly apparitions in photographs.

Interaction: Some ghost tours encourage active participation, such as using ghost-hunting equipment, dowsing rods, or pendulums to detect paranormal activity.

Group Size: Ghost tours vary in group size, so you can choose one that suits your preferences, whether you prefer a more intimate experience or a larger group.

Reservations: It's advisable to make reservations in advance, as popular ghost tours can fill up quickly, especially during peak tourist seasons.

Weather Considerations: Be prepared for varying weather conditions, as Ybor City can be hot and humid. Dress appropriately and bring water if necessary.

Safety: Follow any safety instructions provided by the tour guides, especially if you're walking through historic areas at night.

A ghost tour of Ybor City offers a unique blend of history, folklore, and the supernatural, creating an unforgettable and spine-tingling experience. Whether you're a believer in the paranormal or simply intrigued by local legends, this tour provides an opportunity to delve into the mysterious and haunted side of Ybor City's past.

40.Visit the Tampa Bay Downs racetrack.

Visiting Tampa Bay Downs racetrack is a thrilling experience for horse racing enthusiasts and those looking for a day of excitement at the track. Here's what you can expect when you visit Tampa Bay Downs:

Live Horse Racing: Tampa Bay Downs hosts live thoroughbred horse racing during its season, which typically runs from late November through early May. Check the racetrack's schedule for race dates and times.

Admission: There is usually an admission fee to enter the racetrack, but the cost may vary depending on the day and special events. Some days offer free admission.

Betting: Experience the excitement of wagering on horse races. Tampa Bay Downs provides various betting options, including win, place, show, exacta, trifecta, and more. You can place bets at betting windows or through self-service kiosks.

Race Programs: Pick up a race program or daily racing form to study the horses, jockeys, trainers, and other essential information to help you make informed betting decisions.

Viewing Areas: The racetrack offers different viewing areas, including grandstands, clubhouses, and private suites. Each provides a unique perspective of the races, and some may include amenities like dining and drinks.

Infield Activities: On select race days, the racetrack may host special events and activities in the infield, such as live music, food trucks, and family-friendly entertainment.

Dining Options: Tampa Bay Downs features several dining options, including trackside cafes, bars, and restaurants. Enjoy a meal or a snack while watching the races.

Themed Race Days: Keep an eye out for themed race days, including Kentucky Derby Day, Tampa Bay Derby Day, and more. These events often feature live music, contests, and festivities.

Simulcast Racing: Outside of the live racing season, Tampa Bay Downs offers simulcast racing, allowing you to bet on and watch races from other tracks around the country and world.

Handicapping Seminars: If you're new to horse racing or want to improve your handicapping skills, consider attending handicapping seminars offered by experts at the racetrack.

Special Events: Tampa Bay Downs occasionally hosts special events, such as charity fundraisers, horse shows, and autograph sessions with jockeys and trainers.

Parking: The racetrack typically provides ample parking, and parking fees may apply depending on the day and event.

Safety: Be mindful of safety rules and guidelines while at the racetrack. Follow any instructions provided by staff, especially if you're close to the track during live races.

Tampa Bay Downs offers a thrilling and entertaining day out for horse racing fans and those looking for a unique sporting experience. Whether you're a seasoned handicapper or a first-time visitor, the racetrack's lively atmosphere and competitive races make for an enjoyable outing.

41.Explore the Museum of Science and Industry (MOSI).

Exploring the Museum of Science and Industry (MOSI) in Tampa, Florida, is an engaging and educational experience that offers a wide range of interactive exhibits and activities for visitors of all ages. Here's what you can expect when you visit MOSI:

Interactive Exhibits: MOSI features a variety of hands-on and interactive exhibits covering a wide range of scientific topics, including astronomy, biology, physics, and technology. These exhibits are designed to engage and educate visitors through interactive displays and demonstrations.

Planetarium Shows: The Saunders Planetarium at MOSI offers captivating astronomy shows that take you on a journey through the cosmos. Learn about stars, planets, and other celestial objects in an immersive and educational setting.

Travel to Tampa Florida

IMAX Dome Theatre: MOSI's IMAX Dome Theatre showcases educational and entertaining films on a massive screen. It's a great way to experience documentaries, science-related films, and nature films in stunning detail.

Kids in Charge!: This special area of the museum is designed specifically for young children and features a wide range of age-appropriate exhibits and activities that encourage exploration, creativity, and learning.

Experiential Learning: MOSI emphasizes experiential learning, allowing visitors to actively participate in experiments, demonstrations, and hands-on activities that make science concepts come to life.

Educational Programs: The museum offers a variety of educational programs, including workshops, summer camps, and special events designed to inspire a love of science and learning in visitors of all ages.

Dinosaur World: Explore a collection of life-sized dinosaur models and learn about the prehistoric world in the Dinosaur World exhibit.

Science Challenges: Test your knowledge and problem-solving skills in the museum's interactive science challenges and puzzles.

Gift Shop: Visit the museum's gift shop for science-related toys, books, and souvenirs.

Cafeteria: MOSI has a cafeteria where you can enjoy a meal or refreshments during your visit.

Accessibility: The museum is designed to be accessible to visitors with disabilities, including wheelchair ramps, elevators, and accessible restrooms.

Hours and Admission: Be sure to check MOSI's official website for current hours of operation, admission prices, and any special events or exhibitions.

MOSI is not only an educational destination but also a fun and engaging place to explore the wonders of science and technology. Whether you're visiting with your family, as part of a school group, or on your own, MOSI offers a stimulating and interactive experience that fosters curiosity and a deeper understanding of the world around us.

42.Go on a Tampa Bay brewery tour.

Embarking on a Tampa Bay brewery tour is a delightful way to explore the region's thriving craft beer scene, sample a variety of unique brews, and learn about the craft beer-making process. Here's what you can expect when you go on a brewery tour in Tampa Bay:

Craft Beer Variety: Tampa Bay is home to numerous craft breweries, each with its own distinctive beers and styles. A brewery tour allows you to taste a wide range of craft beers, from IPAs and stouts to sours and lagers.

Tour Options: There are several ways to experience a brewery tour. Some tours provide guided visits to multiple breweries in one day, while others focus on a single brewery's operations. You can choose a tour that matches your preferences and interests.

Behind-the-Scenes Tours: Most brewery tours include a behind-the-scenes look at the brewing process. You'll learn about the ingredients, equipment, and techniques that go into crafting beer, from mashing and fermenting to bottling or canning.

Tasting Sessions: Expect to enjoy tasting sessions during the tour, where you'll sample a selection of the brewery's beers. Knowledgeable guides or brewery staff often provide insights into the flavors and characteristics of each beer.

Local Brewers: Brewery tours offer a chance to meet local brewers and staff who are passionate about their craft. They're often eager to share their knowledge and answer any questions you have.

Souvenirs: Many brewery tours provide branded glassware or other souvenirs as part of the experience. It's a great way to take home a memento of your visit.

Food Pairings: Some brewery tours offer food pairings with beer tastings, enhancing the flavors and creating a more immersive tasting experience.

Educational Aspect: You'll gain a deeper understanding of the art and science behind brewing beer, including the role of hops, yeast, and malt, as well as the importance of fermentation and aging.

Brewery Atmosphere: Experience the ambiance of the breweries themselves, which often feature unique decor, music, and a vibrant atmosphere.

Responsible Tasting: Be mindful of responsible alcohol consumption. Most tours encourage moderation and offer alternatives for those who prefer non-alcoholic options.

Designated Driver Options: If you're traveling with a group, consider having a designated driver who can enjoy the brewery tour without sampling the alcoholic beverages.

Reservations: It's advisable to make reservations for brewery tours, especially during weekends and peak tourist seasons, as they can fill up quickly.

Tampa Bay's craft beer scene is known for its creativity and innovation, making it an excellent destination for beer enthusiasts and anyone interested in the art of brewing. A brewery tour not only provides a taste of local flavors but also a deeper appreciation for the craftsmanship and community behind the craft beer industry.

43.Attend the Florida State Fair.

Attending the Florida State Fair is a fun and immersive experience that offers a wide array of attractions, entertainment, food, and agricultural exhibits. Here's what you can expect when you attend the Florida State Fair:

Dates and Location: The Florida State Fair typically takes place in February and runs for about 11 days. It is held at the Florida State Fairgrounds in Tampa, providing a central location for visitors from across the state.

Admission: Tickets to the fair are available for purchase, and pricing may vary depending on factors such as age, date of visit, and special promotions. Children, seniors, and military personnel often receive discounted rates.

Agricultural Exhibits: Explore the heart of the fair, where you'll find livestock shows, educational displays, and agricultural exhibits. Learn about Florida's farming and ranching heritage and see farm animals up close.

Entertainment: The fair offers a wide range of entertainment options, including live music performances, circus acts, magic shows, and more. Check the fair's schedule for the lineup of daily entertainment.

Amusement Rides: Enjoy thrilling amusement rides, including roller coasters, Ferris wheels, and classic carnival attractions. Individual ride tickets or unlimited ride wristbands are available for purchase.

Fair Food: Indulge in classic fair food favorites such as funnel cakes, corn dogs, cotton candy, deep-fried treats, and a variety of international and exotic foods. The fair is known for its diverse culinary offerings.

Midway Games: Test your skills at the midway games and win prizes. From ring toss to shooting galleries, there are games for all ages.

Exhibits and Competitions: Explore exhibits showcasing art, photography, crafts, and more. The fair often hosts competitions for artists, bakers, gardeners, and other enthusiasts.

Concerts and Entertainment: Check the fair's schedule for live concerts featuring a mix of musical genres, including country, rock, pop, and more. Some concerts may require a separate ticket purchase.

Special Events: The Florida State Fair often features special theme days and events, such as Senior Day, Student Day, and Military and Veterans Appreciation Day, offering discounts and unique activities.

Petting Zoos and Animal Encounters: Bring the family to petting zoos and animal encounters where you can interact with various animals, including exotic species.

Shopping: Browse through vendor booths and marketplace areas offering a wide range of products, from handmade crafts to unique gifts.

Fireworks: Some evenings may conclude with spectacular fireworks displays, providing a grand finale to your fair experience.

Parking: The fairgrounds typically offer parking for a fee, so plan accordingly. Consider carpooling or using alternative transportation options.

Safety: Be mindful of safety guidelines and follow any posted rules and regulations to ensure a safe and enjoyable visit.

Attending the Florida State Fair is a beloved tradition for many Floridians and visitors alike. It offers a blend of entertainment, education, and family-friendly fun, making it a memorable outing for people of all ages. Whether you're interested in agriculture, amusement rides, fair food, or live entertainment, the Florida State Fair has something for everyone to enjoy.

44. Visit the SS American Victory Mariners' Memorial and Museum Ship.

Visiting the SS American Victory Mariners' Memorial and Museum Ship in Tampa, Florida, is a unique and educational experience that allows you to step back in time and explore the history of maritime commerce and the contributions of mariners during World War II. Here's what you can expect when you visit this historic museum ship:

Historic Ship: The SS American Victory is a fully operational Victory-class cargo ship that was built during World War II. It's one of the few remaining ships of its kind in the United States and has been preserved as a museum.

Guided Tours: Explore the ship on a guided tour led by knowledgeable docents who share fascinating stories and insights about the ship's history, its role during the war, and the life of mariners aboard.

Ship Layout: The museum ship is extensive, and you'll have the opportunity to explore various sections, including the engine room, crew quarters, mess halls, cargo holds, and the bridge. You'll gain a deep appreciation for the conditions and challenges faced by mariners during wartime.

Exhibits: Throughout the ship, you'll find informative exhibits, artifacts, and displays that provide a detailed look at the ship's history, the maritime industry, and the experiences of the men and women who served on board.

Interactive Displays: Some areas of the ship feature interactive displays, allowing visitors to engage with the history and operations of the vessel.

Maritime Heritage: The museum ship is a tribute to the American maritime heritage, and you'll learn about the critical role played by merchant mariners in transporting goods and supplies during World War II.

Scenic Views: Climb to the top deck of the ship to enjoy scenic views of Tampa's waterfront, including the skyline and nearby attractions.

Events and Programs: The SS American Victory hosts special events, educational programs, and activities throughout the year, so check the museum's website for updates on what's happening during your visit.

Gift Shop: Visit the museum's gift shop to purchase maritime-themed souvenirs, books, and memorabilia.

Accessibility: The museum ship is generally wheelchair accessible, with ramps and elevators in place to facilitate access.

Hours and Admission: Be sure to check the museum's official website for current hours of operation, admission prices, and any special events or exhibitions.

Visiting the SS American Victory Mariners' Memorial and Museum Ship provides a unique opportunity to appreciate the history and sacrifices of the maritime industry and the men and women who served as mariners during World War II. It's a fascinating journey into the past and an important tribute to the contributions of these unsung heroes of the sea.

45.Explore the International Plaza and Bay Street shopping mall.

Exploring the International Plaza and Bay Street shopping mall in Tampa, Florida, offers a premier shopping and dining experience in a luxurious and stylish setting. Here's what you can expect when you visit this upscale shopping destination:

High-End Retailers: International Plaza is home to a wide array of high-end and luxury retailers, including fashion brands, designer boutiques, jewelry stores, and upscale department stores. Shop for the latest fashion trends, accessories, and more.

Variety of Stores: Whether you're looking for designer clothing, fine jewelry, electronics, home goods, or cosmetics, you'll find a diverse selection of stores to explore.

Bay Street: Bay Street is a vibrant and pedestrian-friendly outdoor district within the mall that features a mix of upscale shops, restaurants, and entertainment venues. It's an ideal place for strolling, people-watching, and enjoying the Florida weather.

Dining Options: International Plaza offers a wide range of dining options, from casual cafes and fast-casual eateries to upscale restaurants. Enjoy a meal, snack, or beverage at one of the many dining establishments throughout the mall.

Luxurious Atmosphere: The mall's interior is designed with an elegant and modern aesthetic, featuring spacious walkways, upscale decor, and natural lighting. It provides a luxurious shopping experience.

Department Stores: Anchor department stores at International Plaza often include Neiman Marcus, Nordstrom, and Dillard's, providing a comprehensive shopping experience.

Specialty Shops: Explore specialty shops that offer unique and one-of-a-kind items, including beauty products, home decor, electronics, and more.

Entertainment: In addition to shopping and dining, International Plaza occasionally hosts live music, events, and entertainment, adding to the vibrant atmosphere.

Seasonal Events: Check the mall's calendar for special events and seasonal promotions, such as holiday celebrations, fashion shows, and exclusive sales.

Concierge Services: The mall may offer concierge services to assist shoppers with inquiries, store information, and services like package delivery and gift wrapping.

Valet Parking: For convenience, consider using valet parking services available at the mall.

Accessibility: International Plaza is designed to be accessible to all visitors, including those with disabilities, with amenities such as ramps, elevators, and accessible restrooms.

Hours of Operation: Be sure to check the mall's official website for current hours of operation and any holiday closures.

Whether you're in search of the latest fashion trends, upscale shopping, fine dining, or simply a place to unwind and explore, the International Plaza and Bay Street shopping mall offers a sophisticated and enjoyable destination. It's a place where you can indulge in retail therapy and experience the upscale side of Tampa's shopping scene.

46.Go hiking in Brooker Creek Preserve.

Hiking in Brooker Creek Preserve is a wonderful way to immerse yourself in the natural beauty and biodiversity of the Tampa Bay area. Located in Tarpon Springs, Florida, this pristine natural preserve offers a variety of hiking trails that wind through a diverse range of ecosystems, making it an ideal destination for nature enthusiasts and outdoor adventurers. Here's what you can expect when you go hiking in Brooker Creek Preserve:

Trail Options: Brooker Creek Preserve features a network of well-maintained hiking trails, each offering a unique experience. The trails vary in length and difficulty, catering to hikers of different skill levels and preferences.

Scenic Beauty: As you hike through the preserve, you'll encounter a lush and picturesque landscape that includes pine flatwoods, hardwood forests, wetlands, and cypress swamps. The scenic beauty of the preserve provides numerous opportunities for wildlife viewing and birdwatching.

Wildlife Viewing: Brooker Creek Preserve is home to a diverse array of wildlife, including white-tailed deer, bobcats, gopher tortoises, and a wide variety of bird species. Keep your eyes peeled for opportunities to spot these animals in their natural habitats.

Educational Signage: Along the trails, you'll find informative signage that offers insights into the local flora, fauna, and ecosystems. Take the time to read and learn about the natural environment you're exploring.

Tranquil Environment: The preserve's peaceful and tranquil environment is a perfect retreat from the hustle and bustle of city life. It's an ideal place to reconnect with nature and enjoy a sense of serenity.

Picnic Areas: Brooker Creek Preserve provides picnic areas where you can enjoy a meal or snack amidst the natural surroundings. Bring a picnic and make it a full day of outdoor adventure.

Dog-Friendly Trails: Some of the trails in the preserve are dog-friendly, allowing you to bring your furry friend along for a hike. Be sure to follow the preserve's pet policies and keep your dog on a leash.

Visitor Center: Before hitting the trails, consider stopping by the preserve's visitor center. It's a valuable resource for obtaining maps, trail information, and additional insights into the preserve's natural history.

Guided Tours: Periodically, the preserve offers guided nature walks and educational programs led by knowledgeable naturalists. Check their schedule for any upcoming events.

Accessibility: Some of the trails in Brooker Creek Preserve are wheelchair accessible or have boardwalks, ensuring that individuals of all abilities can enjoy the natural beauty.

Leave No Trace: Practice Leave No Trace principles by respecting the environment, staying on designated trails, and packing out all trash and litter.

Hours and Regulations: Be aware of the preserve's operating hours, as well as any specific regulations, closures, or seasonal considerations. Always follow the rules to protect the natural habitat.

Hiking in Brooker Creek Preserve offers a rewarding outdoor experience, allowing you to connect with Florida's natural beauty and observe its unique ecosystems. Whether you're interested in a leisurely stroll or a more challenging hike, the preserve provides a serene and captivating setting for exploration and appreciation of the natural world.

47. Visit the Leepa-Rattner Museum of Art in Tarpon Springs.

Visiting the Leepa-Rattner Museum of Art in Tarpon Springs, Florida, is an opportunity to immerse yourself in a diverse collection of art and cultural exhibits. This museum is dedicated to modern and contemporary art, offering visitors a chance to explore the works of significant artists and gain insights into the world of visual arts. Here's what you can expect when you visit the Leepa-Rattner Museum of Art:

Art Collections: The museum houses a diverse range of art collections, including paintings, sculptures, and mixed-media pieces from the 20th and 21st centuries. These collections encompass various artistic movements and styles, providing a rich tapestry of artistic expression.

Permanent Collection: The Leepa-Rattner Museum features a permanent collection that includes works by artists such as Abraham Rattner, Esther Gentle, and Allen Leepa. The collection showcases the evolution of modern and contemporary art and its impact on culture and society.

Rotating Exhibitions: In addition to its permanent collection, the museum hosts rotating exhibitions that feature works by both established and emerging artists. These exhibitions often focus on specific themes, artists, or artistic movements.

Educational Programs: The museum offers educational programs and activities for visitors of all ages. These programs may include art workshops, lectures, guided tours, and interactive exhibits designed to enhance your understanding and appreciation of art.

Interactive Displays: Some exhibits in the museum feature interactive displays and multimedia elements that provide a deeper understanding of the artistic process and the context of the artworks.

Outdoor Sculpture Garden: The museum's outdoor sculpture garden allows you to enjoy art in a natural setting. Stroll through the garden and admire a collection of outdoor sculptures.

Gift Shop: The museum typically has a gift shop where you can purchase art-related merchandise, books, and unique gifts.

Visitor Center: The museum's visitor center provides helpful information, maps, and guidance to ensure you make the most of your visit.

Accessibility: The Leepa-Rattner Museum is designed to be accessible to all visitors, including those with disabilities, with features like ramps, elevators, and accessible restrooms.

Hours and Admission: Check the museum's official website for current hours of operation, admission prices, and any special events or exhibitions.

Guidelines: Follow any guidelines or rules provided by the museum staff, such as photography policies and visitor conduct, to ensure a respectful and enjoyable experience.

Visiting the Leepa-Rattner Museum of Art offers a chance to immerse yourself in the world of modern and contemporary art, appreciate the creative expression of talented artists, and gain a deeper understanding of the role of art in our society. Whether you're an art enthusiast or simply looking for cultural enrichment, this museum provides a captivating and enriching experience.

48.Take a scenic flightseeing tour.

Taking a scenic flightseeing tour in Tampa, Florida, or the surrounding areas is an exhilarating way to gain a unique perspective of the region's natural beauty, landmarks, and coastal vistas. Here's what you can expect when you embark on a scenic flightseeing tour:

Panoramic Views: Enjoy breathtaking panoramic views of the Tampa Bay area, including the city skyline, coastline, and nearby natural attractions. Flightseeing tours provide an unparalleled vantage point from the sky.

Variety of Tours: Flightseeing tours come in various options, including helicopter tours, seaplane tours, and small aircraft tours. Choose the one that suits your preferences and desired experience.

Aerial Landmarks: Depending on the tour you select, you may have the opportunity to see iconic landmarks such as the Sunshine Skyway Bridge, Davis Islands, Tampa's historic districts, and the pristine waters of the Gulf of Mexico.

Wildlife Spotting: Keep an eye out for wildlife such as dolphins, manatees, and schools of fish swimming in the crystal-clear waters below. Flightseeing tours often provide opportunities for wildlife spotting.

Photography: Bring your camera or smartphone to capture stunning aerial photographs of the landscapes, landmarks, and coastal scenes. Flightseeing tours offer incredible photo opportunities.

Narration: Many flightseeing tours include narration by experienced pilots or guides who provide interesting information about the sights you're seeing and the history of the region.

Customizable Tours: Some tour operators offer customizable tours, allowing you to tailor the experience to your interests and preferences. You can request specific routes or destinations.

Safety: Flightseeing tour operators prioritize safety, with well-maintained aircraft, experienced pilots, and adherence to safety regulations. Listen to any safety instructions provided before the flight.

Reservations: It's advisable to make reservations for your flightseeing tour in advance, especially during peak tourist seasons, to secure your preferred date and time.

Weather Considerations: Flightseeing tours are subject to weather conditions. Be prepared for potential changes or rescheduling due to weather-related issues.

Duration: Flightseeing tours can vary in duration, with options for short, scenic flights to longer, more comprehensive tours. Choose the one that fits your schedule.

Accessibility: Confirm the accessibility options for your chosen tour, as some aircraft may have limitations for passengers with mobility challenges.

Group Size: Flightseeing tours can accommodate various group sizes, from private tours for couples to larger groups. Consider your group's size and preferences when booking.

Taking a scenic flightseeing tour offers an unforgettable and perspective-altering experience. It allows you to see familiar places from a new angle while appreciating the beauty of Tampa and its surrounding areas from the sky. Whether you're celebrating a special occasion, seeking adventure, or simply looking to explore the region in a unique way, a flightseeing tour provides an exhilarating and memorable adventure.

49.Explore the Sulphur Springs Museum and Heritage Center.

Exploring the Sulphur Springs Museum and Heritage Center in Tampa, Florida, is an opportunity to delve into the rich history and cultural heritage of the Sulphur Springs neighborhood. This museum and heritage center is dedicated to preserving and sharing the stories, artifacts, and memories of the community. Here's what you can expect when you visit the Sulphur Springs Museum and Heritage Center:

Historical Exhibits: The museum features a range of historical exhibits that showcase the history and development of Sulphur Springs, from its early days as a health resort and spa to its growth as a thriving neighborhood.

Artifacts and Memorabilia: Explore a collection of artifacts, photographs, documents, and memorabilia that provide insights into the lives, experiences, and achievements of Sulphur Springs residents throughout the years.

Interactive Displays: Some exhibits may offer interactive displays and multimedia elements, enhancing your understanding of the neighborhood's history and its significance within the broader context of Tampa.

Oral Histories: The museum may include oral history recordings and interviews with longtime residents, allowing you to hear firsthand accounts and personal stories of Sulphur Springs' past.

Community Engagement: The Sulphur Springs Museum and Heritage Center often hosts community events, workshops, and educational programs that foster engagement and participation among visitors.

Local Art: Look for displays of local art and creative works that celebrate the culture and artistic expressions of Sulphur Springs residents.

Educational Resources: The museum may offer educational resources for schools, researchers, and individuals interested in delving deeper into the history of the neighborhood.

Gift Shop: Visit the museum's gift shop to purchase unique souvenirs, books, and locally crafted items.

Special Events: Check the museum's calendar for special events, exhibitions, and cultural celebrations that may be taking place during your visit.

Hours and Admission: Be sure to check the museum's official website or contact them directly for current hours of operation, admission prices, and any special events or exhibitions.

Guided Tours: Guided tours led by knowledgeable docents may be available to provide additional insights and context to the exhibits. Inquire about guided tour options when you visit.

Accessibility: The museum typically strives to be accessible to all visitors, including those with disabilities, with features such as ramps, accessible restrooms, and accommodations for mobility challenges.

Visiting the Sulphur Springs Museum and Heritage Center offers an opportunity to connect with the cultural heritage and history of this vibrant neighborhood within Tampa. It's a chance to gain a deeper appreciation for the people, events, and stories that have shaped the community over time. Whether you're a history enthusiast, a local resident, or simply curious about the past, this museum provides a meaningful and educational experience.

50.Go deep-sea fishing in the Gulf of Mexico.

Going deep-sea fishing in the Gulf of Mexico is an exciting and adventurous activity that allows you to experience the thrill of reeling in big catches from the depths of the ocean. Here's what you can expect when you embark on a deep-sea fishing adventure in the Gulf of Mexico:

Variety of Species: The Gulf of Mexico is teeming with a diverse range of fish species, including grouper, snapper, kingfish, mahi-mahi, tuna, sailfish, marlin, and more. Depending on the season and location, you may have the chance to catch a variety of fish.

Experienced Captains: Deep-sea fishing charters are typically led by experienced captains and crew members who are knowledgeable about the best fishing spots, techniques, and safety protocols. They will guide you throughout the trip.

Equipment and Gear: Fishing charters provide all the necessary fishing equipment and gear, including fishing rods, reels, bait, and tackle. You'll have access to high-quality equipment to increase your chances of success.

Travel to Tampa Florida

Scenic Views: While out on the Gulf, you'll enjoy scenic views of the open water, the coastline, and possibly even marine wildlife like dolphins, sea turtles, and seabirds.

Catch and Release or Keep: Depending on local regulations and your preferences, you can choose to catch and release the fish you catch or keep them for consumption. Be sure to follow fishing regulations and size limits.

Food and Beverages: Some fishing charters offer food and beverages on board, so you can enjoy a meal or snacks during your fishing excursion. Check with the charter operator about their amenities.

Fishing Techniques: Depending on the target species, you'll use various fishing techniques such as trolling, bottom fishing, and deep-drop fishing. The crew will provide guidance on the best approach for your trip.

Duration: Deep-sea fishing trips can vary in duration, from a half-day trip to a full-day adventure. Choose the trip length that suits your schedule and fishing goals.

Comfort: Fishing charters often provide comfortable amenities on board, including shaded areas, seating, and restroom facilities. Check with the charter operator to understand what amenities are available.

Booking: It's advisable to book your deep-sea fishing trip in advance, especially during peak fishing seasons, as charters can fill up quickly.

Safety: Safety is a top priority on fishing charters. Listen to the captain's safety instructions, wear provided life jackets if required, and follow all safety protocols.

Fishing License: Depending on your location and the charter, you may need to purchase a fishing license. Check with the charter operator to ensure compliance with local regulations.

Deep-sea fishing in the Gulf of Mexico offers an opportunity for anglers of all skill levels to enjoy a thrilling and rewarding experience. Whether you're a seasoned angler or a first-time fisherman, the Gulf's waters provide a chance to catch impressive fish and create memorable fishing stories to share. It's an adventure that combines the excitement of the open sea with the thrill of the catch.

51.Visit the Tampa Bay Automobile Museum.

Visiting the Tampa Bay Automobile Museum in Tampa, Florida, is a unique and fascinating experience for automotive enthusiasts and anyone interested in the history and evolution of automobiles. This museum showcases a collection of vintage and rare automobiles that span different eras of automotive design and innovation. Here's what you can expect when you visit the Tampa Bay Automobile Museum:

Historical Vehicles: The museum houses a diverse collection of automobiles, each representing a specific era, country of origin, or unique engineering and design concepts. You'll have the opportunity to see vehicles from the early 20th century to more recent models.

Educational Exhibits: The museum offers educational exhibits and displays that provide insights into the evolution of automotive technology, design, and engineering. Learn about the innovations that have shaped the automotive industry over the years.

Rare and Uncommon Cars: Many of the cars in the museum's collection are rare or uncommon, showcasing the craftsmanship and creativity of automotive engineers and designers from around the world.

Guided Tours: Guided tours may be available, allowing you to gain a deeper understanding of the museum's collection and the stories behind each vehicle. Knowledgeable guides can provide interesting anecdotes and historical context.

Interactive Displays: Some exhibits may include interactive displays or multimedia elements that enhance your learning experience and allow you to explore the mechanics and features of the vehicles.

Rotating Exhibits: The museum periodically updates its collection with rotating exhibits, ensuring that there's always something new and exciting to see during return visits.

Photography: Bring your camera to capture photographs of these beautifully preserved and restored automobiles. The museum's unique setting provides excellent photo opportunities.

Accessibility: The museum typically strives to be accessible to all visitors, including those with disabilities, with features like ramps, accessible restrooms, and accommodations for mobility challenges.

Gift Shop: Check out the museum's gift shop, where you can find automotive-themed souvenirs, books, and memorabilia.

Hours and Admission: Be sure to check the museum's official website for current hours of operation, admission prices, and any special events or exhibitions.

Community Events: The Tampa Bay Automobile Museum may host community events, car shows, or educational programs related to automobiles and automotive history. Check their event calendar for updates.

Car Enthusiast Gatherings: Some car clubs and car enthusiast groups use the museum as a meeting point or organize events in partnership with the museum. Keep an eye out for gatherings of fellow automotive enthusiasts.

Visiting the Tampa Bay Automobile Museum is like stepping back in time and witnessing the evolution of automobiles, from the early days of automotive engineering to more modern and innovative designs. Whether you have a passion for cars or simply appreciate the art and science of automotive design, this museum offers an engaging and educational experience. It's a place where you can marvel at the beauty and engineering marvels of bygone eras.

52.Attend a Tampa Bay Storm arena football game.

Attending a Tampa Bay Storm arena football game was a thrilling experience for fans of arena football. The Tampa Bay Storm was a professional arena football team that competed in the Arena Football League (AFL) before suspending operations in 2017. While the team is no longer active, here's what you could have expected when attending one of their games:

Fast-Paced Action: Arena football is known for its high-scoring and fast-paced style of play. The games take place in indoor arenas with smaller fields, creating an intense and exciting atmosphere.

Fan Engagement: The Tampa Bay Storm had a dedicated fan base, and attending a game meant being part of the passionate crowd. Fans often engaged in cheers, chants, and energetic support for their team.

Close-Up Experience: The smaller arena size allows fans to be close to the action. You could have been just a few rows away from the players, providing an up-close view of the game.

Halftime Entertainment: Arena football games often feature entertaining halftime shows, including dance performances, contests, and interactive activities to keep fans engaged during breaks in the action.

Family-Friendly Atmosphere: Tampa Bay Storm games were known for their family-friendly environment, making them a great outing for people of all ages.

Affordable Tickets: Arena football games typically offered reasonably priced tickets, making it accessible for fans to enjoy professional football in person.

Autograph Opportunities: Some games provided opportunities for fans to meet players, get autographs, and take photos.

Concessions: Enjoy a variety of food and beverage options at the arena's concessions stands, including classic game-day fare like hot dogs, popcorn, and nachos.

Merchandise: Team merchandise, including jerseys, hats, and other memorabilia, was often available for purchase at the games.

Game Themes: Some games featured special themes or promotions, such as "Military Appreciation Night," "Youth Football Night," or "Fan Appreciation Night."

Accessibility: Most arena football venues are designed to be accessible to all fans, including those with disabilities.

Game Announcements: Listen to the enthusiastic game announcements and commentary to stay informed about the plays and game statistics.

While the Tampa Bay Storm is no longer active, the arena football experience was a memorable and enjoyable one for fans who had the opportunity to support their team. If you're interested in attending arena football games in the future, you may want to explore other arena football teams in different cities that are part of various leagues and continue to provide this exciting form of indoor football entertainment.

53.Explore Lettuce Lake Park.

Exploring Lettuce Lake Park in Tampa, Florida, offers a peaceful and scenic outdoor experience in a natural setting. This park is known for its lush landscapes, wildlife viewing opportunities, and recreational activities. Here's what you can expect when you visit Lettuce Lake Park:

Nature Trails: Lettuce Lake Park features a network of well-maintained nature trails that wind through a variety of ecosystems, including hardwood forests, wetlands, and swamps. These trails offer both paved and unpaved options, making them suitable for walkers, hikers, and cyclists of various skill levels.

Wildlife Viewing: The park is a haven for wildlife enthusiasts. Keep an eye out for native birds, turtles, alligators, and other wildlife that call the park home. Observation towers and boardwalks provide excellent vantage points for birdwatching and animal watching.

Boardwalks: Elevated boardwalks and observation platforms allow you to explore the park's wetlands and cypress swamps up close. These structures provide unique views of the natural habitat and are particularly popular for wildlife photography.

Picnic Areas: Lettuce Lake Park offers picnic areas equipped with tables and grills, making it an ideal spot for a family picnic or a leisurely outdoor meal.

Playgrounds: The park features playgrounds for children, providing a safe and fun space for kids to play and enjoy the outdoors.

Fishing: Anglers can cast their lines from the fishing pier or along the riverbank. The park is known for its diverse fish population, including catfish, bass, and bluegill.

Canoeing and Kayaking: Bring your canoe or kayak to explore the Hillsborough River, which flows through the park. Paddling along the river allows you to appreciate the natural beauty of the area from a different perspective. Canoe and kayak rentals may be available on-site.

Visitor Center: The park's visitor center provides educational exhibits, information on local flora and fauna, and helpful resources for visitors. It's a great place to start your visit and learn more about the park's natural history.

Educational Programs: Lettuce Lake Park often hosts educational programs, nature walks, and guided tours led by park rangers and naturalists. These programs provide insights into the park's ecosystems and wildlife.

Accessibility: The park aims to be accessible to all visitors, with features such as accessible restrooms, ramps, and designated parking spaces.

Bicycling: Biking is permitted on designated trails within the park, making it a great destination for cyclists.

Hours and Admission: Check the park's official website for current hours of operation, admission fees (if applicable), and any special events or programs.

Lettuce Lake Park offers a serene escape from the city, allowing visitors to connect with nature, explore diverse ecosystems, and enjoy outdoor recreational activities. Whether you're interested in birdwatching, hiking, picnicking, or simply immersing yourself in the tranquility of the natural world, this park provides a beautiful and rejuvenating experience.

54. Take a scenic drive to Tarpon Springs.

Taking a scenic drive to Tarpon Springs from Tampa, Florida, is a delightful way to explore the Gulf Coast and experience the charm of this historic and culturally rich town. Here's a suggested route and some points of interest along the way:

Route: Tampa to Tarpon Springs via FL-589 N (Suncoast Parkway)

Distance: Approximately 30 miles (48 kilometers)

Driving Time: Approximately 40-45 minutes, depending on traffic and stops.

Scenic Drive Highlights:

Suncoast Parkway: Begin your scenic drive by heading north on FL-589 N, also known as the Suncoast Parkway. This toll road offers a smooth and picturesque route through the Florida landscape. You'll pass through stretches of greenery and conservation areas.

Anclote River Park: Consider making a stop at Anclote River Park, located along the Anclote River just before reaching Tarpon Springs. The park features a fishing pier, picnic areas, and beautiful riverfront views. It's a great place to stretch your legs and enjoy the serene surroundings.

Historic Downtown Tarpon Springs: As you enter Tarpon Springs, you'll encounter the historic downtown area. This charming district is known for its Greek heritage, sponge docks, and vibrant atmosphere. Park your car and explore the picturesque streets, filled with colorful buildings, shops, and restaurants.

Sponge Docks: Tarpon Springs is famous for its sponge industry. Stroll along the sponge docks area, where you can browse shops selling sponges, Greek imports, and souvenirs. You'll also find numerous Greek restaurants offering delicious cuisine.

Tarpon Springs Sponge Docks Cruise: To get a unique perspective of Tarpon Springs, consider taking a sponge docks cruise. These guided boat tours provide insights into the sponge industry and take you along the Anclote River and Gulf of Mexico.

Greek Bakeries and Cafes: Don't miss the opportunity to sample Greek pastries, baklava, and coffee at one of the local Greek bakeries or cafes in Tarpon Springs.

Tarpon Springs Aquarium: If you're traveling with family, the Tarpon Springs Aquarium is a fun stop to learn about local marine life and see some unique exhibits.

Howard Park Beach: Before heading back to Tampa, you can relax at Howard Park Beach, located a short drive from the downtown area. Enjoy the Gulf Coast's sandy shores, swim in the calm waters, or have a beachside picnic.

Historic Sites: Tarpon Springs also has historic churches and museums that offer insights into the town's rich history and culture.

Art Galleries: If you're interested in art, you may want to explore some of the local art galleries in Tarpon Springs.

This scenic drive from Tampa to Tarpon Springs is not only an opportunity to enjoy the natural beauty of the Gulf Coast but also to immerse yourself in the vibrant Greek culture and history of this unique town. Be sure to take your time to savor the sights, flavors, and experiences along the way.

55.Visit the Tampa Bay Downs Golf Practice Facility.

Visiting the Tampa Bay Downs Golf Practice Facility in Tampa, Florida, is an excellent way to work on your golf game or simply enjoy some recreational golf practice. This facility, associated with the Tampa Bay Downs racetrack and golf course, offers various amenities for golfers of all skill levels. Here's what you can expect when you visit the Tampa Bay Downs Golf Practice Facility:

Driving Range: The practice facility typically includes a spacious driving range with multiple hitting bays. It's a place where you can practice your full swing, work on your accuracy, and fine-tune your distance control.

Putting Greens: Putting is a crucial aspect of golf, and the facility usually features well-maintained putting greens where you can focus on your short game, including putting and chipping.

Chipping Areas: In addition to putting greens, there may be designated chipping and pitching areas where you can practice your approach shots and bunker play.

Golf Instruction: The facility may offer golf instruction and lessons led by experienced golf professionals. Whether you're a beginner looking to learn the basics or an experienced golfer seeking to improve your game, lessons can be a valuable investment.

Club Rental: If you don't have your own golf clubs, check if the facility offers club rental services. This is convenient for travelers or those trying golf for the first time.

Covered Hitting Bays: Some practice facilities have covered or shaded hitting bays, providing relief from the sun or inclement weather.

Equipment and Pro Shop: You can often find a pro shop on-site where you can purchase golf balls, gloves, tees, and other golf accessories you may need for your practice session.

Hours and Rates: Be sure to check the practice facility's hours of operation and pricing. Many facilities offer both daily and membership rates, allowing you to choose the option that suits your needs.

Golf Events: The facility may host golf events, clinics, or tournaments, providing opportunities for socializing with fellow golfers and putting your skills to the test.

Golf Course Access: If you're interested in playing a round of golf after practicing, inquire about access to the Tampa Bay Downs Golf Course, which is often adjacent to the practice facility.

Golf Simulator: Some facilities have golf simulators that allow you to play virtual rounds of golf on famous courses from around the world.

Visiting a golf practice facility like Tampa Bay Downs Golf Practice Facility is an excellent way to enhance your golf skills, enjoy the outdoors, and have a relaxing time on the greens. Whether you're a serious golfer looking to improve your game or a casual player seeking some recreational fun, these facilities offer a welcoming and conducive environment for honing your golfing abilities.

56.Attend the Gasparilla Music Festival.

The Gasparilla Music Festival is a highly anticipated annual music and arts festival held in Tampa, Florida. This vibrant event celebrates a diverse range of musical genres, local art, and the rich cultural tapestry of the Tampa Bay area. Here's what you can expect when attending the Gasparilla Music Festival:

Live Music: The festival showcases a dynamic lineup of musical acts spanning various genres, including rock, indie, jazz, blues, hip-hop, and more. You can enjoy performances by both national and local artists across multiple stages.

Eclectic Music Choices: Gasparilla Music Festival aims to cater to a wide range of musical tastes, so you can expect to hear everything from emerging artists to well-known headliners.

Local Talent: The festival often prioritizes local talent, providing a platform for Tampa Bay's burgeoning music scene. It's a great opportunity to discover new artists and bands.

Food and Beverages: The festival features a diverse selection of food vendors, food trucks, and beverage stations. You can savor a variety of culinary delights, including local and international cuisines, craft beers, and cocktails.

Arts and Crafts: In addition to music, the festival typically includes an arts and crafts village where you can explore and purchase handmade artwork, jewelry, and unique creations from local artisans.

Family-Friendly Activities: Gasparilla Music Festival is often family-friendly, offering activities for children and families, such as interactive art installations, games, and kid-friendly performances.

Community Engagement: The festival fosters a sense of community and often partners with local nonprofit organizations, promoting awareness and support for various causes.

Environmental Sustainability: Many festivals, including Gasparilla Music Festival, prioritize eco-friendly practices, such as recycling, reducing waste, and promoting sustainability.

Art Installations: You'll find eye-catching art installations and exhibits throughout the festival grounds, contributing to the overall creative and immersive atmosphere.

Interactive Experiences: Some festivals offer interactive experiences, such as photo booths, art installations, and themed areas, adding an extra layer of entertainment.

VIP and Premium Experiences: Festival-goers may have the option to purchase VIP or premium tickets that offer exclusive access, amenities, and viewing areas.

Music Workshops and Panels: Some festivals host music workshops, panels, and discussions, providing educational opportunities and insights into the music industry.

Safety and Security: Festival organizers prioritize the safety and security of attendees, with measures in place to ensure a secure and enjoyable experience.

Tickets: Be sure to check the official Gasparilla Music Festival website for ticket information, pricing, and any updates on performers and event details.

Gasparilla Music Festival is a lively and culturally rich event that brings together music lovers, art enthusiasts, and the Tampa Bay community. It offers a chance to experience the city's vibrant music scene, indulge in delicious food and drinks, and immerse yourself in the creative and festive atmosphere. If you plan to attend, consider checking the festival's website for the most up-to-date information on performers, schedules, and logistics to make the most of your experience.

57.Go camping at Fort De Soto Park.

Camping at Fort De Soto Park in Pinellas County, Florida, offers a memorable outdoor experience along the Gulf Coast. Known for its natural beauty, white sandy beaches, and historical sites, Fort De Soto Park is a popular destination for camping enthusiasts. Here's what you can expect when camping at Fort De Soto Park:

Campground Options:

Family Campground: This campground offers 238 campsites suitable for tents, RVs, and trailers. Most sites provide water and electrical hookups, and there are modern restroom facilities with showers. The family campground is located near North Beach, providing easy access to the beach and recreational activities.

Arrowhead Campground: The Arrowhead Campground is a more rustic option with 15 campsites nestled in a wooded area. These sites are well-suited for tent camping and offer a more secluded and natural setting.

Hiking and Biking Trails: Fort De Soto Park features several miles of hiking and biking trails that wind through scenic landscapes, including mangrove forests, saltwater marshes, and beachside paths. Explore the trails and enjoy nature walks and wildlife viewing.

Fishing and Boating: The park offers excellent opportunities for fishing, with options for both freshwater and saltwater angling. You can also launch your boat or kayak from designated areas and explore the park's waterways.

Birdwatching: Fort De Soto Park is a birdwatcher's paradise. Bring your binoculars and camera to observe a variety of bird species, including shorebirds, wading birds, and raptors.

Historical Sites: Explore the historical aspects of the park, including the remnants of Fort De Soto, a Spanish-American War-era fort. The fort's ruins provide a glimpse into the region's history.

Beach Activities: Spend your days on the park's pristine beaches, swimming in the Gulf of Mexico, sunbathing, and building sandcastles. The beaches are known for their soft, white sand and clear waters.

Picnicking: Enjoy picnics at designated areas with picnic tables, grills, and beautiful views. It's a great way to savor meals in a natural setting.

Wildlife Viewing: Keep an eye out for native wildlife, including dolphins, manatees, sea turtles, and a variety of bird species. You may even spot a gopher tortoise, a protected species that inhabits the park.

Campfire Rings: Some campsites in the family campground provide campfire rings, allowing you to enjoy a traditional campfire experience. Be sure to check the availability and regulations for campfires during your visit.

Reservations: Camping at Fort De Soto Park is in high demand, so it's advisable to make reservations well in advance. You can check availability and make reservations on the park's official website or through the county's reservation system.

Camping at Fort De Soto Park provides a serene and picturesque escape, whether you're seeking relaxation on the beach, outdoor adventures, or a chance to connect with nature. It's a fantastic destination for families, couples, and solo travelers alike, offering a balance of natural beauty, historical interest, and recreational opportunities along the Florida Gulf Coast.

58. Visit the Tampa Bay Firefighters Museum.

Visiting the Tampa Bay Firefighters Museum in Tampa, Florida, is an opportunity to explore the rich history of firefighting in the region and gain insight into the courageous efforts of firefighters who have served their community. Here's what you can expect when you visit the Tampa Bay Firefighters Museum:

Historical Exhibits: The museum features a collection of historical artifacts, equipment, and memorabilia related to firefighting in the Tampa Bay area. You can explore exhibits that showcase the evolution of firefighting technology and techniques over the years.

Antique Fire Engines: One of the highlights of the museum is the display of antique fire engines and firefighting equipment. These well-preserved vehicles provide a glimpse into the past and the challenges firefighters faced in battling fires.

Interactive Displays: Some exhibits may include interactive displays and educational elements that engage visitors of all ages. These displays can help you understand the science and art of firefighting.

Firefighter Stories: Learn about the heroic efforts of firefighters who have served the Tampa Bay community. The museum often shares stories and profiles of local firefighters and their contributions.

Educational Programs: The Tampa Bay Firefighters Museum may offer educational programs, workshops, and demonstrations related to fire safety and prevention. These programs are particularly valuable for children and families.

Gift Shop: Check out the museum's gift shop, where you can find firefighter-themed merchandise, souvenirs, and educational materials.

Accessibility: The museum typically strives to be accessible to all visitors, including those with disabilities, with features like ramps, accessible restrooms, and accommodations for mobility challenges.

Events: The museum may host special events, fundraisers, and activities throughout the year. Check their website or contact them directly for information on upcoming events.

Hours and Admission: Be sure to check the museum's official website or contact them for current hours of operation, admission prices, and any special exhibitions or events.

Guided Tours: Guided tours led by knowledgeable docents may be available, providing additional insights and stories about the history of firefighting in the Tampa Bay area.

Visiting the Tampa Bay Firefighters Museum is an opportunity to appreciate the dedication and bravery of firefighters who have served and continue to serve the community. It's also a chance to explore the history of firefighting and gain a deeper understanding of the challenges and triumphs faced by these local heroes. Whether you have a personal connection to firefighting or simply an interest in local history, this museum provides a meaningful and educational experience.

59.Explore the Tampa Bay Watch Bay Discovery Center.

Exploring the Tampa Bay Watch Discovery Center in Tierra Verde, Florida, offers a unique opportunity to learn about the delicate ecosystem of Tampa Bay and the efforts to protect and preserve it. Here's what you can expect when you visit the Tampa Bay Watch Bay Discovery Center:

Educational Exhibits: The Discovery Center typically features a variety of interactive and informative exhibits that highlight the diverse ecosystems found in Tampa Bay. Learn about the bay's marine life, plant species, and the importance of coastal habitats.

Aquariums: You'll likely find aquariums showcasing native marine species, providing an up-close look at the bay's underwater inhabitants. These aquariums are both educational and visually captivating.

Hands-On Activities: The center often offers hands-on activities and educational programs suitable for visitors of all ages. These activities may include touch tanks, interactive displays, and workshops focused on marine science and conservation.

Environmental Stewardship: Tampa Bay Watch is dedicated to environmental stewardship, and the Discovery Center serves as a hub for raising awareness about the bay's health and promoting sustainable practices. Learn how you can contribute to preserving this vital ecosystem.

Virtual and Guided Tours: Depending on the availability, you may have the option to join virtual or guided tours of the Discovery Center. These tours can provide in-depth insights into the bay's ecology and conservation efforts.

Outdoor Spaces: The center may include outdoor areas where you can enjoy scenic views of Tampa Bay and observe local wildlife. These spaces often have educational signage to help you identify different species.

Educational Programs: Tampa Bay Watch frequently hosts educational programs and events related to marine conservation, environmental science, and coastal restoration. Check their schedule for upcoming programs and activities.

Volunteer Opportunities: If you're passionate about environmental conservation, inquire about volunteer opportunities with Tampa Bay Watch. They often organize community cleanup events and restoration projects.

Gift Shop: Many environmental centers have gift shops where you can purchase environmentally friendly products, books, and souvenirs that support the organization's mission.

Accessibility: The center typically aims to be accessible to all visitors, with features such as ramps, accessible restrooms, and accommodations for mobility challenges.

Hours and Admission: Be sure to check the Discovery Center's official website for current hours of operation, admission fees (if applicable), and any special programs or events.

Visiting the Tampa Bay Watch Bay Discovery Center is an educational and inspiring experience, providing insights into the delicate balance of marine ecosystems and the importance of conservation efforts in protecting Tampa Bay. It's an ideal destination for families, students, nature enthusiasts, and anyone interested in learning about the natural wonders of the bay and the role we can play in its preservation.

60.Attend the Tampa Bay International Dragon Boat Races.

Attending the Tampa Bay International Dragon Boat Races is a thrilling and culturally rich experience that allows you to witness the excitement of dragon boat racing, a sport with ancient origins. Here's what you can expect when attending this event:

Dragon Boat Racing: The focal point of the event is the dragon boat races themselves. Teams from around the world compete in colorful, long, narrow boats adorned with dragon heads and tails. Each boat is manned by a crew of paddlers who work in unison to propel the boat forward.

Team Spirit: Dragon boat racing is not only a sport but also a celebration of teamwork, camaraderie, and cultural heritage. You can expect to see teams dressed in matching uniforms, often with unique team names and logos.

Cultural Performances: The Tampa Bay International Dragon Boat Races often feature cultural performances, including traditional dances, music, and martial arts demonstrations. These performances provide insights into the rich cultural traditions of the participating teams.

Food and Refreshments: Explore food vendors offering a variety of cuisines, including both international and local dishes. It's a great opportunity to savor delicious food and beverages from different cultures.

Crafts and Souvenirs: Look for vendors selling crafts, souvenirs, and dragon boat-themed merchandise. You can find everything from clothing and accessories to artwork and trinkets.

Interactive Activities: Some events may offer interactive activities for attendees, such as paddleboard lessons, boat rides, or cultural workshops.

Children's Activities: Family-friendly dragon boat festivals often include activities for children, such as face painting, games, and storytelling.

Cultural Exhibits: Explore cultural exhibits and displays that provide insights into the history, art, and traditions of the participating teams.

Dragon Boat Education: Learn about the history and significance of dragon boat racing through educational exhibits and informational displays.

Spectator Viewing: Find a comfortable spot along the waterfront or designated spectator area to watch the races. The excitement of the paddlers, the drummers' rhythmic beats, and the colorful dragon boats make for a captivating spectacle.

Dragon Boat Drummers: Each dragon boat typically has a drummer who sets the pace and rhythm for the paddlers. Their role is not only essential to the race but also adds to the visual and auditory spectacle.

Awards and Ceremonies: Attend award ceremonies where winning teams are recognized and celebrated. It's a chance to cheer for your favorite teams and appreciate their achievements.

Community Involvement: Dragon boat festivals often have a strong sense of community involvement, with proceeds from the event often supporting local charities or cultural organizations.

Accessibility: Many dragon boat festivals aim to be accessible to all attendees, with provisions for people with disabilities and family-friendly facilities.

Festival Atmosphere: Immerse yourself in the festive atmosphere, complete with music, cheering spectators, and the vibrant energy of the event.

The Tampa Bay International Dragon Boat Races provide an exciting blend of sport, culture, and entertainment. Whether you're a dragon boat enthusiast, a cultural explorer, or simply looking for a fun and dynamic event, this festival offers a unique and memorable experience. Be sure to check the event's official website or contact the organizers for information on event dates, schedules, and any specific activities or performances planned for the year you plan to attend.

61.Go on a Segway tour of Tampa.

Taking a Segway tour of Tampa is a fun and unique way to explore the city's landmarks and attractions while gliding effortlessly on a Segway personal transporter. Here's what you can expect when you embark on a Segway tour of Tampa:

Training Session: Most Segway tours begin with a brief training session to ensure that all participants are comfortable and confident riding a Segway. Guides will teach you how to operate the Segway safely and efficiently.

Expert Guide: You'll be accompanied by an experienced and knowledgeable tour guide who will lead the way, provide information about the city's history and culture, and ensure a smooth and enjoyable tour experience.

Scenic Routes: Segway tours typically follow scenic routes that showcase the best of Tampa's landmarks and neighborhoods. You'll have the opportunity to see iconic sites and hidden gems along the way.

Landmarks: Depending on the tour route, you may pass by or stop at notable landmarks such as the Tampa Riverwalk, Tampa Bay History Center, Curtis Hixon Waterfront Park, and more.

Historical Information: Guides often share historical tidbits and interesting facts about Tampa's past, adding depth to your understanding of the city.

Photo Opportunities: The Segway tour will likely include stops at key points of interest, allowing you to take photos and capture memories of your journey.

Group Experience: Segway tours are a popular group activity, making them a great option for families, friends, and team-building outings. You can share the experience with fellow participants.

Customized Tours: Some Segway tour operators offer customized tours based on your interests and preferences. Whether you're interested in history, architecture, or specific neighborhoods, you can often tailor the tour to your liking.

Safety: Safety is a top priority during Segway tours. Guides will provide helmets and ensure that participants are following safety guidelines throughout the tour.

Duration: Tour lengths vary, so you can choose a tour that fits your schedule and interests. Some tours are as short as one hour, while others may be longer.

Evening Tours: Some operators offer evening Segway tours, allowing you to experience the city's nightlife and illuminated landmarks.

Reservation: It's a good idea to make a reservation in advance, especially during peak tourist seasons or if you have a specific date and time in mind.

Accessibility: Segway tours are generally accessible to most participants, but it's a good idea to check with the tour operator regarding any mobility or health concerns.

Riding a Segway is a fun and eco-friendly way to explore Tampa's vibrant streets, historic areas, and scenic waterfront. Whether you're a first-time rider or a Segway enthusiast, these tours offer an engaging and memorable way to discover the city's culture and attractions. Be sure to check with local Segway tour providers for the latest information on available tours, schedules, and any safety guidelines.

62. Visit the Upper Tampa Bay Trail.

Visiting the Upper Tampa Bay Trail is a wonderful way to explore the natural beauty of the Tampa Bay area and enjoy outdoor activities like walking, jogging, biking, and wildlife viewing. Here's what you can expect when you visit the Upper Tampa Bay Trail:

Scenic Trail: The Upper Tampa Bay Trail is a well-maintained, scenic trail that winds through natural landscapes, offering a peaceful and enjoyable experience for outdoor enthusiasts.

Trail Length: The trail is approximately 7.25 miles long, making it ideal for a leisurely stroll, a long run, or a bike ride. The flat and paved surface is suitable for all fitness levels.

Shaded Areas: You'll find shaded sections along the trail, which can be especially welcome on hot Florida days. These shaded areas provide a cool respite as you explore.

Wildlife Viewing: Keep an eye out for local wildlife such as birds, butterflies, and squirrels. The trail passes through habitats like wetlands and forests, providing opportunities for wildlife observation.

Rest Areas: There are rest areas along the trail with benches and picnic tables where you can take a break, enjoy a snack, or simply soak in the natural surroundings.

Dog-Friendly: The trail is dog-friendly, so you can bring your furry companion for a walk or run. Just be sure to keep your dog on a leash and clean up after them.

Biking: The trail is also popular among cyclists. Bikers can enjoy a dedicated lane for a smooth and safe ride.

Family-Friendly: The trail is suitable for families with children. It's a great place for a family bike ride or a nature walk where kids can learn about local flora and fauna.

Fitness Stations: Some sections of the trail feature fitness stations with exercise equipment, allowing you to incorporate strength and stretching exercises into your outdoor workout.

Accessibility: The trail is typically designed to be accessible to individuals with disabilities, including those using wheelchairs or mobility aids.

Restrooms and Water Fountains: Look for restrooms and water fountains at various points along the trail, providing convenience for visitors.

Trail Maps: Trail maps and information are often available at the trailhead, helping you plan your route and explore different sections of the trail.

Sunset Viewing: The trail is a popular spot for watching sunsets over the bay. Be sure to check the local sunset times and plan your visit accordingly for a breathtaking view.

Safety: Safety is a priority, and the trail is usually well-lit in the evenings. It's a safe place for outdoor activities, but it's always a good idea to follow safety guidelines and be aware of your surroundings.

The Upper Tampa Bay Trail is a serene escape from the hustle and bustle of city life, offering a peaceful natural setting where you can connect with the outdoors, stay active, and enjoy the beauty of the Tampa Bay area. Whether you're a local looking for a regular outdoor exercise spot or a visitor seeking a tranquil nature walk, this trail provides a welcoming and rejuvenating experience.

63.Attend the Tampa Bay Black Heritage Festival.

Attending the Tampa Bay Black Heritage Festival is a celebration of African American culture, history, and contributions to the Tampa Bay community. This annual event typically features a diverse range of activities, performances, and educational opportunities. Here's what you can expect when attending the Tampa Bay Black Heritage Festival:

Cultural Performances: Enjoy live music, dance performances, spoken word poetry, and other artistic expressions that celebrate African American culture and heritage. Performances often feature local and nationally recognized artists.

Educational Exhibits: Explore exhibits and displays that highlight African American history, achievements, and contributions to the Tampa Bay area and beyond. These exhibits may cover topics such as civil rights, art, literature, and more.

Art and Crafts: Browse through art galleries and craft booths featuring the work of African American artists and artisans. You can often find unique artwork, jewelry, clothing, and other handmade items.

Food and Cuisine: Savor delicious soul food and traditional African American dishes at food vendors and food trucks. It's an opportunity to indulge in a variety of flavors and culinary traditions.

Health and Wellness: The festival may include health and wellness screenings, workshops, and discussions focused on promoting health and well-being within the African American community.

Community Engagement: Engage with local organizations, community leaders, and nonprofits that work to address important social and cultural issues facing the African American community.

Children's Activities: Family-friendly activities and entertainment are often available, including interactive workshops, games, and storytelling for children.

Historical Reenactments: Some festivals feature historical reenactments that bring pivotal moments in African American history to life.

Lectures and Workshops: Attend lectures, workshops, and panel discussions on topics related to African American culture, history, and contemporary issues.

Vendor Marketplace: Shop at a marketplace where vendors offer clothing, accessories, books, and other items that celebrate African American heritage.

Parades and Processions: Depending on the festival's schedule, you may have the opportunity to participate in or watch parades and processions featuring vibrant costumes and cultural expressions.

Community Awards: Many festivals recognize outstanding individuals and organizations for their contributions to the African American community through awards and ceremonies.

Live Entertainment: Enjoy a lineup of live entertainment that may include gospel music, jazz, R&B, and other genres that have had a significant impact on African American culture.

Networking: Connect with fellow attendees and community members who share an interest in celebrating and preserving African American heritage.

Dates and Location: Check the official website of the Tampa Bay Black Heritage Festival for the most up-to-date information on event dates, locations, schedules, and any special guests or performers.

The Tampa Bay Black Heritage Festival provides a platform to honor the rich history and cultural diversity of the African American community. It's an opportunity to learn, celebrate, and embrace the contributions and achievements of African Americans while enjoying a lively and festive atmosphere. Whether you have a personal connection to the culture or simply want to immerse yourself in a vibrant cultural celebration, this festival offers a meaningful and enjoyable experience.

64. Explore the Channel District.

Exploring the Channel District in Tampa, Florida, is an exciting urban adventure that offers a blend of entertainment, dining, waterfront views, and cultural attractions. Located near downtown Tampa and the Port of Tampa, the Channel District has evolved into a vibrant neighborhood with plenty to see and do. Here's what you can expect when exploring the Channel District:

Travel to Tampa Florida

Amalie Arena: The district is home to the Amalie Arena, an iconic sports and entertainment venue where you can catch Tampa Bay Lightning hockey games, concerts, and other live events. The arena's exterior features striking architecture and is worth admiring.

Sparkman Wharf: This bustling waterfront district within the Channel District offers a variety of dining options, bars, and entertainment. You can enjoy outdoor seating, live music, and a diverse culinary scene, all with beautiful views of Tampa Bay.

The Florida Aquarium: Located adjacent to the Channel District, The Florida Aquarium is a must-visit attraction. Explore diverse marine life exhibits, interactive displays, and even have the chance to swim with sharks in a controlled environment.

Tampa Riverwalk: Stroll along the scenic Tampa Riverwalk, which connects the Channel District to downtown Tampa and other neighborhoods. The Riverwalk features public art installations, parks, and stunning views of the Hillsborough River.

Cruise Ports: The Port of Tampa is nearby, making it convenient if you're embarking on a cruise. The district often bustles with activity when cruise ships are in port.

Channelside Bay Plaza: This shopping and dining complex offers additional choices for entertainment, shopping, and dining. It's a popular spot to grab a meal or enjoy a drink before or after an event at Amalie Arena.

Tampa Bay History Center: Located just a short walk from the Channel District, the Tampa Bay History Center provides insights into the area's rich history, including exhibits on early settlers, pirates, and the maritime heritage of Tampa Bay.

Public Art: Keep an eye out for public art installations and sculptures throughout the district. These artworks add to the neighborhood's character and cultural appeal.

Water Activities: Enjoy water-based activities like kayaking, paddleboarding, or taking a boat tour from the nearby docks. You can explore the waterfront and take in scenic views of the city.

Nightlife: As the sun sets, the Channel District comes to life with a vibrant nightlife scene. Explore bars, lounges, and clubs for an evening of entertainment and socializing.

Residential Living: The Channel District is a thriving residential area with luxury condominiums and apartments. Some visitors choose to stay in accommodations here to be close to the action.

Events: Check the local event calendar for special events, festivals, and activities that may be happening in the Channel District during your visit.

The Channel District is a dynamic and evolving neighborhood that provides a unique blend of urban amenities, waterfront charm, and cultural attractions. Whether you're attending an event at Amalie Arena, exploring the waterfront, or enjoying the dining and entertainment options, the Channel District offers a lively and enjoyable urban experience in Tampa.

65.Go on a casino cruise.

Going on a casino cruise is an entertaining and unique way to enjoy gaming, dining, and entertainment while cruising on the beautiful waters of the Gulf of Mexico or Tampa Bay. Here's what you can typically expect when embarking on a casino cruise in the Tampa area:

Gaming: Casino cruises offer a variety of gaming options, including slot machines, table games like blackjack and roulette, poker, and more. Whether you're a novice or an experienced gambler, there are games to suit all levels of expertise.

Dining: Most casino cruises feature onboard dining options, including buffets, restaurants, and snack bars. You can enjoy a meal while taking in scenic views of the water.

Entertainment: Casino cruises often host live entertainment, such as music, shows, and performances. The onboard entertainment enhances the overall experience and provides an opportunity to relax between gaming sessions.

Drinks and Bars: Cruise ships typically have bars and lounges where you can order a variety of beverages, including cocktails, wine, beer, and non-alcoholic options.

Travel to Tampa Florida

Scenic Views: As you cruise along the water, you'll have the opportunity to take in stunning coastal views, sunsets, and the natural beauty of the Gulf of Mexico or Tampa Bay.

Events and Promotions: Check the cruise operator's schedule for special events, promotions, and themed cruises. Some cruises may offer discounts, giveaways, or tournaments.

Casino Classes: If you're new to casino gaming, some cruises offer classes or tutorials to help you learn the rules and strategies of popular casino games.

Gaming Packages: Many cruise operators offer gaming packages that include perks such as casino credits, food and drink vouchers, and entertainment tickets.

Age and Identification: Be aware that there may be age restrictions to enter the casino area, typically 18 or 21 years of age, depending on the cruise operator's policies. You'll also need to present a valid ID.

Reservations: It's a good idea to make reservations in advance, especially during peak seasons or on weekends, as casino cruises can be popular and fill up quickly.

Duration: Casino cruises vary in duration, with some lasting a few hours and others offering overnight trips. Choose a cruise that suits your schedule and preferences.

Dress Code: Check the cruise operator's dress code, as some may have specific requirements for attire, especially in dining areas.

Please note that the availability and specifics of casino cruises can vary, so it's advisable to check with the specific cruise operator for the most up-to-date information on schedules, prices, and offerings. Whether you're looking for a night of gaming excitement, a unique dining experience, or simply a relaxing cruise on the water, a casino cruise in the Tampa area can provide an enjoyable and memorable outing.

66.Attend the Tampa International Gay and Lesbian Film Festival.

Attending the Tampa International Gay and Lesbian Film Festival (TIGLFF) is a fantastic way to celebrate LGBTQ+ cinema and culture while enjoying a diverse selection of films, events, and discussions. Here's what you can typically expect when attending TIGLFF:

Film Screenings: TIGLFF showcases a curated selection of LGBTQ+ films from around the world, including feature films, documentaries, shorts, and experimental works. These films explore a wide range of themes and perspectives within the LGBTQ+ community.

Filmmaker Q&A: After many screenings, you'll have the opportunity to engage with filmmakers and actors during Q&A sessions. It's a chance to gain insights into the creative process and the stories behind the films.

Panel Discussions: TIGLFF often hosts panel discussions and forums on LGBTQ+ topics, including social issues, representation in media, and the arts. These discussions provide a platform for dialogue and community engagement.

Awards and Recognitions: The festival may include award ceremonies that honor outstanding films, filmmakers, and contributors to LGBTQ+ cinema.

Opening and Closing Night Galas: TIGLFF often kicks off and concludes with glamorous galas, featuring live entertainment, dancing, food, and drinks. These events create a festive atmosphere and an opportunity to socialize with fellow festivalgoers.

Special Events: Look for special events like themed parties, art exhibitions, and performances that complement the film festival experience.

Community Engagement: TIGLFF is more than just a film festival; it's a community celebration. Attendees often include LGBTQ+ individuals, allies, activists, and cinephiles who come together to share stories and celebrate diversity.

Networking: Connect with fellow film enthusiasts, LGBTQ+ advocates, and industry professionals. The festival provides a welcoming and inclusive environment for networking and building connections.

Youth and Student Programs: Some festivals offer youth and student programs that focus on LGBTQ+ issues and filmmaking. These programs can be educational and empowering for younger attendees.

Accessibility: TIGLFF typically strives to be accessible to all attendees, including those with disabilities. Be sure to check with the festival organizers for specific accessibility accommodations.

Ticketing and Passes: Purchase tickets or festival passes in advance to secure your access to screenings and events. Passes often provide cost-effective access to multiple films and activities.

Dates and Locations: Check the official TIGLFF website or event announcements for the most up-to-date information on festival dates, screening venues, and program schedules.

TIGLFF is not only a celebration of LGBTQ+ cinema but also an opportunity to engage with important social issues, connect with the LGBTQ+ community, and enjoy outstanding films from diverse perspectives. Whether you're a film enthusiast, an advocate for LGBTQ+ rights, or someone seeking an inclusive and vibrant cultural experience, attending TIGLFF can be an enriching and inspiring journey.

67. Visit the Tampa Bay Aviation Association.

The Tampa Bay Aviation Association is a valuable resource and organization for aviation enthusiasts, professionals, and individuals interested in the aviation industry in the Tampa Bay area. Here's what you can typically expect when visiting or getting involved with the Tampa Bay Aviation Association:

Networking Opportunities: The association often hosts networking events, meetings, and gatherings where aviation professionals and enthusiasts can connect, share experiences, and build relationships within the industry.

Educational Programs: Look for educational programs, seminars, and workshops that cover various aspects of aviation, including safety, technology, and industry trends. These programs provide valuable insights and knowledge.

Community Engagement: The Tampa Bay Aviation Association may be involved in community outreach efforts related to aviation education, career development, and safety initiatives. They often collaborate with local schools and organizations to promote aviation.

Advocacy and Promotion: The association may engage in advocacy efforts to promote the growth and sustainability of the aviation industry in the Tampa Bay region. They may advocate for policies and initiatives that benefit the local aviation community.

Industry Updates: Stay informed about the latest developments and news in the aviation industry, both locally and nationally, through newsletters, publications, and events organized by the association.

Awards and Recognitions: The association may recognize outstanding individuals or organizations that have made significant contributions to the aviation field through awards and ceremonies.

Membership Benefits: Consider becoming a member of the Tampa Bay Aviation Association to access exclusive benefits, such as discounts on events, access to industry resources, and opportunities for professional growth.

Engaging Events: The association often hosts events related to aviation, which may include airshows, fly-ins, aviation career fairs, and more. These events provide opportunities for hands-on experiences and interaction with aircraft.

Youth and Education: Some associations are involved in initiatives that encourage young people to pursue careers in aviation. This may include scholarships, mentorship programs, and educational resources.

Access to Aviation Facilities: Depending on the association's affiliations, you may have access to aviation facilities, hangars, or airports in the Tampa Bay area for tours or special events.

Community Support: By participating in the Tampa Bay Aviation Association, you contribute to the growth and vitality of the local aviation community and help support the industry's presence in the region.

Collaboration: The association often collaborates with other aviation organizations, industry partners, and governmental agencies to address common challenges and opportunities in aviation.

To visit the Tampa Bay Aviation Association or get involved, you can typically check their official website for information on upcoming events, membership details, and contact information. Whether you're a pilot, aviation enthusiast, student pursuing an aviation career, or simply curious about aviation, the Tampa Bay Aviation Association can provide a welcoming and informative community to connect with fellow aviation enthusiasts and professionals in the region.

68.Go on a brewery bike tour.

Going on a brewery bike tour in Tampa is a delightful way to explore the city's craft beer scene while enjoying a leisurely bike ride. Tampa has a thriving craft brewery culture, and a bike tour allows you to visit multiple breweries, taste a variety of brews, and soak in the local atmosphere. Here's what you can typically expect when embarking on a brewery bike tour in Tampa:

Guided Tour: Most brewery bike tours are guided by knowledgeable tour leaders who are passionate about craft beer and the local brewing scene. They provide insights into the breweries, the brewing process, and the history of Tampa's beer culture.

Bike Rental: If you don't have your own bike, the tour operator typically provides bike rentals. These bikes are often equipped for a comfortable ride, and helmets may also be provided.

Brewery Visits: The tour will include stops at several local breweries, each offering a unique selection of craft beers. You'll have the opportunity to taste various styles of beer, from IPAs to stouts, lagers, and more.

Tastings: At each brewery stop, you'll enjoy tastings of their featured beers. Some tours may include a flight of samples, while others offer full pints or a combination of both.

Behind-the-Scenes: Depending on the brewery and tour, you may get a behind-the-scenes look at the brewing process, with explanations of how beer is made and the chance to chat with brewers.

Local Insights: Tour guides often share local history, fun facts, and stories related to the breweries and the neighborhoods you visit.

Bike-Friendly Routes: The tour route is usually designed to be bike-friendly, with safe and scenic paths or roads that connect the breweries. It's a fun way to explore the city while staying active.

Snacks and Water: Some tours provide snacks or water to keep you refreshed and energized during the ride.

Souvenirs: Depending on the tour, you may receive a souvenir such as a branded pint glass, bottle opener, or other brewery-related merchandise.

Safety: Safety is a top priority, and tour leaders typically ensure that participants follow safe biking practices throughout the tour.

Group Size: Tours can vary in group size, from small intimate tours to larger groups. Be sure to check with the tour operator for details on group size and availability.

Duration: Brewery bike tours can range in duration, typically lasting a few hours. Some may offer half-day or full-day options.

Custom Tours: Some tour operators offer customizable tours, allowing you to select specific breweries or neighborhoods to visit based on your preferences.

Age Restrictions: Be aware that brewery tours often have age restrictions, and participants must be of legal drinking age to enjoy the beer tastings.

Reservations: It's advisable to make reservations in advance, as brewery bike tours can be popular and may have limited availability.

Brewery bike tours provide a fun and interactive way to explore Tampa's craft beer scene, meet fellow beer enthusiasts, and discover new favorite brews. Whether you're a seasoned craft beer aficionado or just beginning to explore the world of craft beer, these tours offer an enjoyable and educational experience in the city.

69.Explore the Curtis Hixon Waterfront Park.

Exploring Curtis Hixon Waterfront Park in Tampa is a delightful way to enjoy outdoor activities, take in beautiful scenery, and experience a vibrant urban park. Located along the Hillsborough River in downtown Tampa, this park offers a range of attractions and amenities for visitors of all ages. Here's what you can typically expect when exploring Curtis Hixon Waterfront Park:

Green Spaces: The park features well-maintained lawns and green spaces where you can relax, have a picnic, play frisbee, or simply enjoy the fresh air and sunshine.

Scenic River Views: Curtis Hixon Park offers stunning views of the Hillsborough River and the Tampa skyline. It's an ideal spot for taking photographs and enjoying waterfront vistas.

Playgrounds: The park often includes playgrounds with equipment for children, making it a family-friendly destination.

Interactive Fountains: Cool off in the park's interactive fountains. These water features are especially popular with children and provide a fun way to beat the Florida heat.

Riverwalk Access: The park is connected to the Tampa Riverwalk, allowing you to take a leisurely stroll or bike ride along the waterfront and explore more of downtown Tampa.

Outdoor Events: Curtis Hixon Waterfront Park hosts a variety of outdoor events throughout the year. These events may include concerts, festivals, food trucks, yoga classes, movie nights, and cultural celebrations.

Art Installations: Keep an eye out for public art installations and sculptures that are often on display within the park, adding to its cultural appeal.

Dog-Friendly: The park may have designated areas where dogs are allowed on-leash, making it a welcoming place for pet owners.

Amphitheater: The park may feature an amphitheater for live performances and events. Check the park's schedule for upcoming shows and concerts.

Food and Beverage: You'll find food vendors, cafes, and restaurants in the vicinity of the park, allowing you to grab a meal or snack before or after your visit.

Fitness: Some visitors use the park for jogging, yoga, or outdoor workouts. It's a great place to stay active.

Community Gatherings: Curtis Hixon Waterfront Park is a hub for community gatherings and special occasions. You may come across weddings, parties, and other celebrations during your visit.

Accessibility: The park is typically designed to be accessible to all visitors, including those with mobility challenges.

Safety: The park is often well-lit, and security measures are in place to ensure a safe environment for visitors.

Public Restrooms: Look for public restrooms, which are often available for convenience.

Curtis Hixon Waterfront Park provides a tranquil and scenic escape in the heart of downtown Tampa. It's a place where you can enjoy the beauty of the river, engage in outdoor activities, and participate in a variety of events and cultural experiences. Whether you're looking for a relaxing afternoon, a family outing, or a lively event, this park offers a welcoming and vibrant urban oasis. Be sure to check the park's schedule for any upcoming events or activities during your visit.

70.Attend the Tampa Greek Festival.

Attending the Tampa Greek Festival is a wonderful way to immerse yourself in Greek culture, savor delicious Greek cuisine, enjoy traditional music and dance, and experience the warmth and hospitality of the Greek community in Tampa. Here's what you can typically expect when attending the Tampa Greek Festival:

Delicious Greek Cuisine: The festival is known for its mouthwatering Greek food offerings. You can savor traditional dishes such as gyro, moussaka, souvlaki, spanakopita (spinach pie), baklava, and many other Greek specialties. There are often options for both meat lovers and vegetarians.

Greek Pastries: Don't miss the opportunity to indulge in a wide array of Greek pastries and desserts, including baklava, loukoumades (honey-dipped donuts), and koulourakia (butter cookies). These sweet treats are often homemade and incredibly delicious.

Live Music and Dance: The festival typically features live Greek music and dance performances. You can watch traditional Greek dances, including the lively and energetic line dances that are a highlight of the event.

Cultural Exhibits: Explore cultural exhibits that showcase Greece's rich history, art, and traditions. Learn about Greek mythology, history, and the significance of various cultural elements.

Marketplace: Browse through a marketplace where vendors offer Greek products, crafts, jewelry, and souvenirs. It's a great place to shop for unique gifts and keepsakes.

Cooking Demonstrations: Some festivals offer cooking demonstrations where you can learn how to prepare Greek dishes at home. These demonstrations often feature expert chefs sharing their culinary secrets.

Children's Activities: The Tampa Greek Festival is family-friendly and often includes activities for children, such as games, face painting, and storytelling.

Church Tours: The festival is often held at or near a Greek Orthodox church, and you may have the opportunity to take guided tours of the church to learn about its architecture and religious significance.

Cultural Presentations: Look for cultural presentations and lectures that delve into Greek history, art, and culture. These presentations can be both informative and entertaining.

Greek Coffee: Enjoy a cup of traditional Greek coffee, known for its strong and rich flavor. It's often served with a piece of baklava or other sweets.

Traditional Attire: Many attendees and volunteers wear traditional Greek clothing, adding to the festive atmosphere.

Greek Wine and Spirits: Some festivals offer a selection of Greek wines, ouzo (an anise-flavored liqueur), and other Greek beverages for those interested in exploring Greek libations.

Outdoor Seating: The festival usually provides outdoor seating areas where you can enjoy your food, listen to music, and soak in the lively atmosphere.

Diverse Entertainment: Depending on the festival's schedule, you may also encounter additional entertainment, such as Greek music bands and cultural performances.

Admission: While admission policies and ticket prices may vary, some festivals offer free admission, while others have a nominal entrance fee.

The Tampa Greek Festival is not only a celebration of Greek culture but also a welcoming and inclusive event that invites everyone to experience the beauty and flavors of Greece. Whether you're of Greek descent or simply interested in exploring a new culture, this festival offers a fun and culturally enriching experience that is sure to leave you with lasting memories and a taste of Greece. Be sure to check the festival's official website for the most up-to-date information on dates, location, and event details.

71.Visit the American Victory Ship Mariners' Memorial Museum.

Visiting the American Victory Ship Mariners' Memorial Museum in Tampa is a fascinating experience that allows you to step back in time and explore a restored World War II cargo ship. This museum provides insights into maritime history, wartime efforts, and the experiences of the men and women who served aboard these vessels. Here's what you can typically expect when visiting the American Victory Ship Mariners' Memorial Museum:

Historic Ship Tour: The main attraction is the SS American Victory, a fully restored Victory-class cargo ship from World War II. Guided tours and self-guided tours are available, allowing you to explore various areas of the ship, including the cargo holds, crew quarters, engine room, and bridge.

Educational Exhibits: The museum features a range of educational exhibits related to the ship's history, the role of cargo ships during WWII, and the experiences of the merchant mariners who sailed aboard them. These exhibits often include artifacts, photographs, and informative displays.

Interactive Displays: Some exhibits are interactive, providing hands-on experiences that help visitors understand the challenges and daily life aboard a cargo ship during wartime.

Veteran Stories: Hear stories and testimonials from veterans who served on similar cargo ships during WWII. Their firsthand accounts provide a personal and emotional connection to the history.

Restoration Efforts: Learn about the extensive restoration work that went into preserving the SS American Victory and the dedication of volunteers who helped bring this historic vessel back to life.

Memorabilia and Artifacts: Explore a collection of maritime memorabilia and artifacts, including items related to navigation, communication, and life at sea during WWII.

Events and Special Programs: Check the museum's calendar for special events, programs, and educational opportunities. These may include lectures, film screenings, and themed events.

Gift Shop: The museum often has a gift shop where you can purchase maritime-themed souvenirs, books, and memorabilia.

Scenic Views: Enjoy scenic views of the Port of Tampa and Tampa Bay from the deck of the ship. It's a great vantage point for taking photographs.

Accessibility: The museum strives to be accessible to all visitors, including those with mobility challenges.

Volunteer Opportunities: Some visitors choose to volunteer at the museum, helping with ongoing restoration efforts, guiding tours, and sharing their passion for maritime history.

Guided Tours: If you prefer a guided tour, knowledgeable docents are available to provide in-depth information and answer questions about the ship and its history.

Hours of Operation: Check the museum's official website for the most up-to-date information on hours of operation, admission fees, and any special events or exhibitions.

Visiting the American Victory Ship Mariners' Memorial Museum is not only an educational experience but also a tribute to the brave men and women who served during WWII and the importance of preserving maritime history. It's a unique opportunity to step aboard a living piece of history and gain a deeper appreciation for the sacrifices made during wartime.

72.Go on a sunset hot air balloon ride.

Going on a sunset hot air balloon ride in the Tampa Bay area is a breathtaking and serene experience that allows you to witness a stunning sunset from the sky. While hot air balloon rides are not typically offered within the city of Tampa itself, there are hot air balloon operators in nearby regions, such as Orlando and Central Florida, that offer sunset rides. Here's what you can generally expect when going on a sunset hot air balloon ride:

Scenic Views: As you ascend into the sky in the hot air balloon's basket, you'll be treated to panoramic views of the surrounding landscapes, which can include lush countryside, lakes, forests, and sometimes even views of the coastline.

Sunset Magic: The highlight of the experience is, of course, watching the sunset from a unique vantage point. The colors of the sky as the sun sets are often awe-inspiring and provide a romantic and serene atmosphere.

Breathtaking Photo Opportunities: Bring your camera or smartphone to capture the stunning vistas and the vibrant colors of the setting sun. Balloon rides offer some of the best aerial photography opportunities.

Tranquil Flight: Hot air balloon rides are known for their peaceful and smooth flights. Unlike other forms of aviation, the experience is quiet and calm, allowing you to fully appreciate the beauty of the landscape below.

Professional Pilots: Your hot air balloon ride will be led by a skilled and certified pilot who will ensure a safe and enjoyable journey. They often share insights about ballooning and the area you're flying over.

Champagne Toast: Many hot air balloon rides conclude with a traditional champagne toast upon landing, adding a touch of elegance to your adventure.

Group or Private Rides: You can choose to embark on a ride as part of a group or arrange for a private ride for a more intimate experience.

Weather-Dependent: Balloon rides are weather-dependent, so it's essential to check the weather conditions before your scheduled flight. Safety is a top priority, and flights may be rescheduled or canceled if conditions are not suitable.

Duration: Sunset hot air balloon rides typically last around one hour, but the entire experience, including preparation and post-flight celebrations, can take a few hours.

Meeting Point: You'll often meet at a designated launch site or meeting point, where the balloon is prepared for flight. After the ride, you'll be transported back to the meeting point or your starting location.

Reservations: Advance reservations are recommended, especially for sunset rides, as they tend to be popular and can fill up quickly.

While you may need to travel a short distance to enjoy a hot air balloon ride, the experience of floating gracefully above the landscape as the sun sets is a memory that you'll cherish. It's a perfect choice for a romantic date, a special occasion, or simply an opportunity to connect with nature and take in the beauty of the world from a different perspective.

73. Explore Fort Foster State Historic Site.

Exploring Fort Foster State Historic Site is like stepping back in time to the era of the Second Seminole War in the 19th century. This well-preserved historic site, located in Thonotosassa, Florida, offers a glimpse into military history and the life of soldiers during that period. Here's what you can typically expect when visiting Fort Foster State Historic Site:

Historical Reenactments: The site often hosts historical reenactments of military life during the Second Seminole War. These events feature costumed reenactors who demonstrate the daily activities, drills, and weaponry of soldiers from that era.

Guided Tours: Joining a guided tour is an excellent way to learn about the history of Fort Foster and its significance during the Seminole Wars. Knowledgeable guides share stories and insights about the fort and the events that took place there.

Self-Guided Exploration: You can also explore the site at your own pace. There are interpretive signs and markers throughout the area to provide information about the structures and history.

Historic Structures: The site features reconstructed buildings and structures that were part of the fort, including barracks, a guardhouse, officers' quarters, and a blockhouse. These buildings are designed to resemble their 19th-century counterparts.

Weapons and Artifacts: Some exhibits showcase period-specific weapons, equipment, and artifacts used by soldiers during the Seminole Wars. This provides a tangible connection to the past.

Nature Trails: Fort Foster is located within Hillsborough River State Park, and you can explore nature trails in the surrounding area. These trails offer opportunities for hiking, wildlife viewing, and enjoying the natural beauty of the park.

Picnic Areas: The park often includes picnic areas and facilities, making it a great place for a family outing or a leisurely lunch during your visit.

Cultural and Educational Programs: Depending on the season, the site may offer educational programs, special events, and cultural activities that further immerse visitors in the history of the fort and the Seminole Wars.

Photography: Fort Foster and the surrounding park provide picturesque settings for photography, whether you're interested in capturing the historic structures, natural landscapes, or wildlife.

Accessibility: Efforts are made to ensure that the site is accessible to all visitors, including those with mobility challenges.

Visitor Center: Check out the visitor center, where you can find additional historical information, exhibits, and maps of the site.

Hours of Operation: Be sure to check the hours of operation and any admission fees, as they may vary depending on the season and special events.

Visiting Fort Foster State Historic Site offers a unique opportunity to connect with Florida's history and gain insights into the challenges and experiences of soldiers during the Seminole Wars. Whether you have a strong interest in history or simply appreciate the chance to explore a well-preserved historic site, Fort Foster provides an educational and enriching experience.

74. Visit the Tampa Bay Automobile Museum.

Visiting the Tampa Bay Automobile Museum is a treat for automotive enthusiasts and history buffs alike. Located in Pinellas Park, Florida, this museum showcases a unique collection of vintage automobiles from the early 20th century to the 1960s, highlighting the evolution of automotive design and engineering. Here's what you can typically expect when visiting the Tampa Bay Automobile Museum:

Historic Automobiles: The museum features a diverse and well-preserved collection of automobiles from different eras. These cars are displayed in chronological order, allowing you to see the evolution of automotive technology and design.

Educational Exhibits: Each automobile is accompanied by detailed information about its history, design, engineering, and technological innovations. The museum provides insights into the development of automotive engineering.

Rare and Unique Models: You'll find rare and unique vehicles that you may not encounter elsewhere. These cars often represent specific design trends or technological breakthroughs of their time.

Thematic Displays: Some exhibits may focus on specific themes, such as innovations in aerodynamics, early electric vehicles, or groundbreaking safety features.

Interactive Displays: The museum occasionally offers interactive displays or hands-on activities that allow visitors to better understand the mechanics and engineering of these vintage automobiles.

Guided Tours: Guided tours led by knowledgeable docents are often available. These tours provide in-depth information about the cars, their historical context, and the stories behind their design.

Photo Opportunities: The museum offers excellent opportunities for photography, whether you're capturing the elegance of classic cars or the intricate details of their craftsmanship.

Accessibility: The museum typically strives to be accessible to all visitors, including those with mobility challenges.

Gift Shop: Check out the museum's gift shop, where you can find automotive-themed merchandise, books, and souvenirs.

Special Events: The Tampa Bay Automobile Museum occasionally hosts special events, lectures, and educational programs related to automotive history and engineering.

Hours of Operation and Admission: Be sure to check the museum's official website or contact them for the most up-to-date information on hours of operation, admission fees, and any special exhibitions.

Visiting the Tampa Bay Automobile Museum is like taking a journey through automotive history. Whether you're an avid car enthusiast, a history lover, or simply curious about the evolution of transportation, this museum offers a captivating and educational experience that celebrates the art and science of the automobile.

75.Go on a Tampa Bay food tour.

Going on a Tampa Bay food tour is a fantastic way to explore the culinary delights of this vibrant Florida region. Tampa Bay is known for its diverse and flavorful food scene, offering a wide range of dishes influenced by various cultures. Here's what you can generally expect when embarking on a Tampa Bay food tour:

Culinary Exploration: Food tours in Tampa Bay typically take you on a culinary journey through various neighborhoods, each known for its unique cuisine and dining establishments.

Expert Guides: Knowledgeable and passionate guides lead the tour, sharing insights into the history, culture, and flavors of the region. They often have insider knowledge about the local food scene.

Travel to Tampa Florida

Diverse Food Tastings: You'll have the opportunity to sample a variety of dishes at multiple stops. These tastings can include appetizers, entrees, desserts, and beverages, allowing you to experience a wide range of flavors.

Local Restaurants: The tour may feature visits to locally-owned restaurants, cafes, food trucks, and eateries. It's a chance to discover hidden gems and support local businesses.

Cultural Insights: Along the way, you'll learn about the cultural influences that have shaped Tampa Bay's cuisine, including Cuban, Spanish, Italian, and more.

Historical Context: Guides often provide historical context and stories about the neighborhoods and establishments you visit, making the tour both informative and entertaining.

Interaction with Chefs and Owners: Some tours offer the opportunity to meet and chat with chefs, restaurant owners, or food artisans, giving you a deeper understanding of the culinary process.

Group Size: Food tour group sizes can vary, but they are typically small to ensure an intimate and personalized experience.

Walking or Trolley Tours: Depending on the tour, you may explore on foot, via a trolley, or using another mode of transportation. Walking tours allow for a leisurely pace and the chance to take in the surroundings.

Local Specialties: You'll have the chance to savor local specialties and dishes that Tampa Bay is known for. This can include Cuban sandwiches, seafood, key lime pie, and more.

Vegetarian and Dietary Options: Many food tours can accommodate dietary restrictions, including vegetarian, vegan, or gluten-free options. Be sure to inform the tour operator of any dietary preferences or allergies in advance.

Duration: Food tours typically last a few hours, allowing you to enjoy a sampling of the best flavors Tampa Bay has to offer.

Reservations: Advance reservations are often required, especially for popular tours, so be sure to book your spot in advance.

Souvenirs: Some tours include a souvenir or memento of your foodie adventure, such as a culinary guide or a gift from one of the visited establishments.

Local Recommendations: Guides often share recommendations for other dining experiences and activities in the area, ensuring you make the most of your visit to Tampa Bay.

Tampa Bay's food tours are a delightful way to savor the region's culinary diversity, learn about its history, and connect with fellow food enthusiasts. Whether you're a local looking to explore your city's food scene or a visitor wanting to taste the flavors of Tampa Bay, a food tour promises a memorable and delicious experience. Be sure to check with the specific food tour operator for details on tour availability, meeting points, and any specific dietary considerations.

76.Attend the Tampa Pig Jig.

The Tampa Pig Jig is an annual barbecue and music festival that combines delicious smoked meats, live music, and a festive atmosphere, all while raising funds for a great cause. Held in Tampa, Florida, the event typically features barbecue competitions, food vendors, live musical performances, and activities for attendees of all ages. Here's what you can expect when attending the Tampa Pig Jig:

Barbecue Competition: The heart of the event is a barbecue cook-off where talented pitmasters and teams compete to create the most mouthwatering smoked meats. You can watch the teams in action and even sample their creations.

Variety of Barbecue: The festival offers a variety of barbecue options, including pulled pork, ribs, brisket, and more. You can enjoy a BBQ feast with your choice of sauces and sides.

Live Music: The Tampa Pig Jig typically hosts live musical performances by well-known bands and artists. The music adds to the festive atmosphere, creating a lively and enjoyable experience.

Family-Friendly Activities: The event often includes family-friendly activities such as games, inflatables, face painting, and interactive entertainment for children.

Travel to Tampa Florida

Craft Beer and Beverages: You can pair your barbecue with craft beers, cocktails, and non-alcoholic beverages available at the festival.

Vendor Marketplace: Browse through a marketplace featuring vendors selling a variety of items, including artisan crafts, clothing, and barbecue-related products.

Cooking Demonstrations: Some festivals offer cooking demonstrations and workshops where you can learn about barbecue techniques and tips from experts.

Benefitting a Cause: The Tampa Pig Jig is not only a celebration of food and music but also a charitable event. The proceeds from the festival often go toward supporting the NephCure Kidney International charity, which funds research and advocacy for kidney disease.

Competitions and Awards: You can witness the barbecue competition results and awards ceremonies, where the best pitmasters and teams are recognized for their culinary skills.

Costumes and Themes: Some attendees and teams participate in the festival's themes and dress up in creative costumes, adding to the festive spirit.

Tickets and Admission: Check the event's official website for ticket information, including pricing, availability, and any age restrictions.

Safety and Security: The festival organizers prioritize safety and often have security measures in place to ensure a safe and enjoyable environment for all attendees.

The Tampa Pig Jig is not only a celebration of barbecue and music but also a community-focused event that supports a meaningful cause. Whether you're a barbecue aficionado, a music lover, or simply looking for a fun day out with family and friends, this festival offers a great opportunity to enjoy delicious food, live entertainment, and the camaraderie of fellow festival-goers, all while contributing to a charitable mission. Be sure to check the event's official website for the most up-to-date information on dates, location, ticketing, and entertainment lineup.

77.Explore the Upper Tampa Bay Trail.

Exploring the Upper Tampa Bay Trail is a wonderful way to enjoy the natural beauty of the Tampa Bay area and engage in outdoor activities. This scenic trail provides an opportunity for hiking, biking, running, and enjoying the great outdoors. Here's what you can typically expect when exploring the Upper Tampa Bay Trail:

Scenic Trail: The Upper Tampa Bay Trail is a multi-use paved trail that winds its way through picturesque landscapes, including wetlands, woodlands, and open fields. It offers a tranquil escape from the urban hustle and bustle.

Trail Length: The trail spans approximately 14 miles, making it suitable for both short leisurely walks and longer recreational journeys.

Biking: Cyclists often use the trail to enjoy a scenic ride through the natural surroundings. The flat and well-maintained surface is ideal for all skill levels, including families with children.

Walking and Running: The trail is also popular among walkers and runners. It provides a safe and peaceful environment for exercise, whether you're strolling at a leisurely pace or training for a race.

Wildlife Viewing: Keep an eye out for local wildlife as you explore the trail. You may spot birds, turtles, and other animals in their natural habitat.

Trailhead Facilities: The trail typically has trailhead facilities with amenities such as parking, restrooms, water fountains, and picnic areas. These amenities make it convenient for visitors to start and finish their journeys comfortably.

Shade and Rest Areas: The trail often includes shaded areas and benches where you can take a break and enjoy the scenery.

Dog-Friendly: Leashed dogs are often allowed on the trail, making it a great place for pet owners to enjoy outdoor activities with their four-legged companions.

Accessibility: Efforts are often made to ensure the trail is accessible to people with disabilities.

Connectivity: The Upper Tampa Bay Trail is part of the larger regional trail system and can connect to other trails and parks in the Tampa Bay area, providing opportunities for longer excursions.

Safety: Safety measures, such as well-marked crosswalks and designated pedestrian and cyclist lanes, are typically in place to ensure a safe experience for all users.

Events and Activities: Some sections of the trail may host special events, group rides, or educational programs throughout the year. Check local event listings for any activities that may coincide with your visit.

Whether you're seeking outdoor exercise, a peaceful nature walk, or a family-friendly biking adventure, the Upper Tampa Bay Trail offers a scenic and well-maintained route for residents and visitors alike. It's a great way to connect with nature, enjoy the Florida sunshine, and experience the natural beauty of the Tampa Bay area. Be sure to bring water, sunscreen, and any necessary gear for your chosen activity, and always follow any posted rules and regulations for trail usage.

78. Visit the Tampa Baseball Museum at the Al Lopez House.

The Tampa Baseball Museum at the Al Lopez House is a must-visit destination for baseball enthusiasts and history buffs. This museum is dedicated to preserving and celebrating the rich baseball heritage of Tampa, Florida, and the legacy of Al Lopez, a legendary Major League Baseball player and manager. Here's what you can typically expect when visiting the Tampa Baseball Museum at the Al Lopez House:

Historical Exhibits: The museum features a wide range of exhibits, artifacts, and memorabilia related to the history of baseball in Tampa, including photographs, uniforms, equipment, and more. It provides a comprehensive look at the city's deep connection to the sport.

Al Lopez Legacy: Learn about the life and career of Al Lopez, a Tampa native who achieved fame as a catcher in the Major Leagues and later as a successful manager. Explore his contributions to the world of baseball and his impact on the Tampa community.

Local Baseball History: Discover the history of baseball in Tampa, from its early beginnings to its role as a spring training destination for Major League teams. Explore the stories of local players, coaches, and teams that have left their mark on the sport.

Interactive Exhibits: Some exhibits may be interactive, allowing visitors to engage with the history and culture of baseball through multimedia displays, audio recordings, and hands-on activities.

Educational Programs: The museum may offer educational programs, workshops, and presentations related to baseball history and culture. Check for any scheduled events during your visit.

Gift Shop: Browse the museum's gift shop for baseball-themed souvenirs, books, apparel, and collectibles.

Guided Tours: Guided tours are often available, providing in-depth insights into the exhibits and the history of baseball in Tampa. Knowledgeable docents share stories and anecdotes about the sport's local significance.

Historic Al Lopez House: The museum is located in the historic Al Lopez House, which is an attraction in itself. The house is a beautifully preserved example of Mediterranean Revival architecture and provides a glimpse into the lifestyle of the era.

Hours of Operation: Check the museum's official website or contact them for the most up-to-date information on hours of operation, admission fees, and any special exhibitions.

Visiting the Tampa Baseball Museum at the Al Lopez House is not just an opportunity to explore the history of baseball but also a chance to appreciate the cultural significance of the sport in Tampa's community. Whether you're a devoted baseball fan or simply curious about the local history, this museum offers a rewarding and informative experience that celebrates the game and its connection to the Tampa Bay area.

79.Attend a Tampa Roller Derby match.

Attending a Tampa Roller Derby match is a thrilling and action-packed experience that combines athleticism, entertainment, and the excitement of roller skating. Roller derby is a fast-paced, full-contact sport, and Tampa Bay is home to a vibrant roller derby community. Here's what you can typically expect when attending a Tampa Roller Derby match:

Roller Derby Basics: Roller derby is played on an oval track, and two teams of roller skaters compete against each other. Each team has a jammer whose goal is to score points by lapping members of the opposing team while the blockers try to stop them.

Family-Friendly Atmosphere: Roller derby matches in Tampa Bay often have a family-friendly atmosphere, making them suitable for attendees of all ages. It's a fun and unique way to spend an evening with friends and family.

Live Action: Roller derby matches are known for their high-energy and physical gameplay. Skaters use strategy and teamwork to gain an advantage, making each match an exciting and dynamic spectacle.

Local Teams: Tampa Bay typically has several roller derby teams, each with its own unique identity and fan base. Popular teams in the area may include the Tampa Roller Derby, the Tampa Bay Bruise Crew, and others.

Affordable Tickets: Tickets to roller derby matches are often reasonably priced, making it an accessible entertainment option. Some events may even offer special deals for groups or season passes.

Concessions: Concession stands or food trucks are often available, so you can enjoy snacks and refreshments while watching the matches.

Merchandise: Support your favorite roller derby team by purchasing team merchandise such as T-shirts, posters, and other fan gear.

Meet and Greet: Some roller derby events allow fans to meet the skaters and learn more about the sport. This can be a great opportunity to connect with the athletes and gain insight into the world of roller derby.

Theme Nights: Some matches may have themed events or special promotions, adding to the festive atmosphere. Themes can range from costume nights to charity fundraisers.

Community Involvement: Roller derby leagues in Tampa Bay often have a strong commitment to community involvement and may participate in charitable activities or volunteer work.

Accessibility: Roller derby venues are typically wheelchair accessible, and accommodations can be made for attendees with disabilities.

Fan Engagement: Get involved in the excitement by cheering for your favorite team, making signs, and enjoying the camaraderie of fellow fans.

Safety: While roller derby is a contact sport, safety measures are in place to protect skaters and ensure a safe and enjoyable experience for spectators.

To attend a Tampa Roller Derby match, check the schedule of local roller derby leagues, and visit their official websites or social media pages for information on upcoming events, tickets, and venues. Roller derby matches are not only a thrilling sports experience but also a celebration of athleticism, teamwork, and community spirit, making them a unique and entertaining outing for residents and visitors alike.

80.Explore Old Tampa Bay.

Exploring Old Tampa Bay offers a glimpse into the rich history, natural beauty, and recreational opportunities that this scenic body of water has to offer. Old Tampa Bay is a portion of Tampa Bay located on the western coast of Florida, and it encompasses a variety of activities and experiences. Here's what you can typically expect when exploring Old Tampa Bay:

Scenic Views: Old Tampa Bay provides stunning waterfront views and serene landscapes. Whether you're on the water or along the shoreline, you can enjoy breathtaking sunsets and the beauty of the bay.

Water Activities: The bay offers various water activities such as boating, kayaking, paddleboarding, and fishing. You can explore the calm waters, mangrove-lined shores, and small islands that dot the bay.

Fishing: Old Tampa Bay is known for its excellent fishing opportunities. Anglers can cast their lines in search of a variety of fish species, including snook, redfish, trout, and more.

Birdwatching: The bay is a haven for birdwatchers. You can spot a diverse range of bird species, including ospreys, herons, pelicans, and wading birds. Birdwatching enthusiasts often visit the bay's natural areas and preserves.

Wildlife Viewing: Beyond birds, Old Tampa Bay is home to various wildlife species, such as dolphins, manatees, and the occasional sea turtle. Keep your eyes peeled for these fascinating creatures.

Parks and Preserves: There are several parks and nature preserves around Old Tampa Bay, providing opportunities for hiking, picnicking, and observing the local flora and fauna. Examples include Cypress Point Park and Mobbly Bayou Wilderness Preserve.

Historical Sites: Explore the historical sites and landmarks that surround Old Tampa Bay. These can include old fishing villages, historical markers, and the remnants of early settlements.

Sunset Cruises: Consider taking a sunset cruise on the bay to witness the sun dipping below the horizon while enjoying a relaxing boat ride.

Culinary Experiences: Several waterfront restaurants and seafood eateries offer delicious dining options with views of Old Tampa Bay. It's an excellent opportunity to savor fresh seafood and local cuisine.

Photography: Old Tampa Bay provides numerous opportunities for photography enthusiasts to capture the natural beauty, wildlife, and coastal scenery.

Environmental Education: Some areas around the bay offer educational programs and exhibits that highlight the bay's ecosystems, conservation efforts, and environmental significance.

Access Points: There are public access points, boat ramps, and marinas located along the bay's shoreline, making it easy for visitors to embark on their chosen water-based adventure.

Events and Festivals: Keep an eye out for local events and festivals that may take place near Old Tampa Bay, including outdoor concerts, seafood festivals, and community gatherings.

Exploring Old Tampa Bay allows you to connect with nature, experience the bay's natural beauty, and immerse yourself in the history and culture of the area. Whether you prefer to spend your time on the water, enjoy outdoor activities, or simply relax by the bay, this picturesque part of Tampa Bay offers a diverse range of experiences for visitors and locals to enjoy.

81.Go on a wildlife eco-tour.

Embarking on a wildlife eco-tour in the Tampa Bay area is a fantastic way to connect with nature, observe local wildlife, and learn about the delicate ecosystems that thrive in the region. These tours typically take you to the best natural habitats and provide opportunities for wildlife viewing while promoting environmental conservation. Here's what you can generally expect when going on a wildlife eco-tour in the Tampa Bay area:

Experienced Guides: Knowledgeable guides, often naturalists or wildlife experts, lead the tours. They provide valuable insights about the local flora and fauna, as well as the conservation efforts in the area.

Eco-Friendly Transportation: Many eco-tours use eco-friendly modes of transportation, such as kayaks, canoes, paddleboards, electric boats, or small, low-impact vessels, to minimize the impact on the environment.

Diverse Habitats: Tours typically visit a variety of natural habitats, including mangrove forests, wetlands, estuaries, rivers, and coastal areas, each with its own unique wildlife.

Wildlife Observation: You'll have the opportunity to observe native wildlife in their natural habitats. This can include dolphins, manatees, shorebirds, alligators, sea turtles, and a variety of fish and bird species.

Educational Component: Eco-tours often have an educational component, where guides share information about the local ecosystems, wildlife behaviors, and the importance of conservation.

Photography Opportunities: Bring your camera or smartphone to capture the stunning natural scenery and the wildlife you encounter along the way.

Interactivity: Some tours may allow you to actively participate in wildlife monitoring efforts, such as tracking and recording animal sightings or collecting data for scientific research.

Customized Experiences: Depending on your interests, some eco-tours offer customizable experiences, such as birdwatching tours, sunset cruises, or educational programs for families.

Group Size: The size of the tour group is often limited to minimize disturbances to wildlife and ensure a more personalized experience.

Safety Measures: Eco-tour operators prioritize safety, often providing life jackets, safety instructions, and ensuring that tours adhere to local regulations.

Seasonal Variations: The best time for wildlife viewing can vary by season, so check with the tour operator to plan your visit during peak wildlife activity.

Responsible Tourism: Many eco-tours promote responsible tourism practices, emphasizing Leave No Trace principles and encouraging participants to respect and protect the natural environment.

Duration: Tours can range from a few hours to full-day excursions, so you can choose an experience that fits your schedule and interests.

Reservation and Pricing: Advance reservations are often recommended, and pricing varies depending on the tour and its duration.

By going on a wildlife eco-tour in the Tampa Bay area, you not only get to experience the natural beauty of the region but also contribute to the conservation and protection of its diverse ecosystems. These tours offer an enriching and educational experience that allows you to connect with nature and appreciate the importance of preserving our natural heritage.

82. Visit the Florida Southern College campus in nearby Lakeland.

Visiting the Florida Southern College (FSC) campus in nearby Lakeland is a delightful experience for those interested in architecture, art, and the beauty of a historic college campus. Known for its stunning architecture designed by famed architect Frank Lloyd Wright, Florida Southern College offers a unique and visually captivating environment. Here's what you can typically expect when visiting the Florida Southern College campus:

Architectural Marvels: FSC is famous for its "Child of the Sun" collection of buildings designed by Frank Lloyd Wright. These structures feature Wright's distinctive organic architecture and include the Annie Pfeiffer Chapel, the Polk County Science Building, the Esplanades, and more. Each building is a work of art in itself.

Guided Tours: The college typically offers guided tours of the campus, allowing visitors to learn about the history, architecture, and significance of each building. Knowledgeable docents provide insights into Wright's design philosophy and the college's history.

Beautiful Grounds: In addition to the iconic buildings, the campus boasts well-maintained gardens, courtyards, and water features. The lush landscape complements the architecture and offers tranquil spaces for leisurely walks and reflection.

Annie Pfeiffer Chapel: The chapel is one of the highlights of the campus, featuring a stunning stained glass "Lego" window design by Wright. Visitors are often welcome to enter the chapel and explore its interior.

Visitor Center: The campus often has a visitor center where you can obtain maps, tour information, and details about the college's history.

Art Exhibits: FSC is known for its commitment to the arts, and you may have the opportunity to visit art galleries or attend cultural events on campus.

Educational Programs: Depending on the time of your visit, there may be educational programs, lectures, or events taking place on campus. Check the college's website for any scheduled activities during your visit.

Photography: The campus provides excellent opportunities for photography, whether you're capturing the architectural details, gardens, or the overall ambiance.

Accessibility: The campus is typically accessible to visitors, including those with mobility challenges. Be sure to check for information on accessible routes and facilities.

Cultural Significance: Learn about the cultural and historical significance of FSC's architecture and its role in the broader context of American architectural history.

Visitor Etiquette: While the campus is open to visitors, it's important to be respectful of the college community and adhere to any posted guidelines or rules.

Visiting the Florida Southern College campus in Lakeland is like stepping into a living work of art. It's an opportunity to appreciate the genius of Frank Lloyd Wright's design and to immerse yourself in the unique atmosphere of this historic institution. Whether you're an architecture enthusiast or simply looking for a serene and culturally enriching outing, a visit to FSC is a memorable experience. Be sure to check the college's official website for visitor information, tour availability, and any specific guidelines for guests.

83. Attend the Tampa Bay Improv Festival.

Attending the Tampa Bay Improv Festival promises a night of laughter, creativity, and spontaneous humor. Improvisational comedy, often referred to as improv, is a form of theater where performers create scenes, characters, and dialogue on the spot, based on audience suggestions. The Tampa Bay Improv Festival typically features a lineup of talented improv groups and troupes from around the region and beyond. Here's what you can typically expect when attending this festival:

Improv Performances: The festival showcases a diverse array of improv performances by skilled improvisers. Each show is unique, as it is created in the moment, and relies on audience participation and suggestions to shape the scenes and humor.

Variety of Styles: You can expect to see various styles of improv, including short-form and long-form improv, musical improv, and experimental formats. Different troupes may bring their own distinctive approaches to the art form.

Audience Interaction: Improv performances often involve audience interaction, with audience members providing suggestions or participating in games and scenes. The level of involvement is typically voluntary and lighthearted.

Comedic Talent: Enjoy the comedic talents of improvisers who excel at quick thinking, wit, and humor. The festival is a great opportunity to discover emerging comedic talent and witness seasoned performers in action.

Workshops and Classes: Some improv festivals offer workshops and classes led by experienced improvisers. These provide an opportunity for attendees to learn about the fundamentals of improv and try their hand at the art form.

Networking: If you're interested in improv or comedy, the festival can be a great place to network with fellow comedy enthusiasts, performers, and instructors.

Comedic Community: Immerse yourself in the local and regional comedic community. You'll likely encounter people who share your passion for humor and comedy.

Festival Atmosphere: The festival often has a lively and celebratory atmosphere. Attendees can enjoy the camaraderie of fellow audience members who appreciate the spontaneity and humor of improv.

Venues: The festival may take place in various venues, such as theaters, comedy clubs, or performing arts spaces. Check the festival's official website or program for details on show locations and schedules.

Ticketing: Be sure to check the festival's website or ticketing platform for information on ticket prices, showtimes, and any special events or packages.

The Tampa Bay Improv Festival offers an opportunity to laugh, be entertained, and appreciate the art of improvisational comedy. Whether you're a fan of comedy or curious about the world of improv, this festival provides a welcoming and enjoyable experience. Be sure to plan ahead, check the festival's official website for the most up-to-date information, and reserve your tickets in advance for a night of spontaneous humor and laughter.

84.Explore the historic Hyde Park Village shopping district.

Hyde Park Village is a charming and historic shopping district located in Tampa, Florida. Nestled in the heart of the Hyde Park neighborhood, this upscale shopping and dining destination offers a mix of boutique shops, eateries, and a welcoming atmosphere. Here's what you can typically expect when exploring the historic Hyde Park Village:

Boutique Shopping: Hyde Park Village is known for its boutique shopping, featuring a curated selection of upscale retailers offering fashion, jewelry, accessories, home goods, and more. You can find unique and stylish items from both national and local brands.

Dining and Cafes: The district is home to a variety of restaurants, cafes, and eateries offering diverse culinary experiences. Whether you're in the mood for a gourmet meal, a casual coffee, or sweet treats, you'll find options to satisfy your palate.

Sidewalk Cafes: Many restaurants in the area have outdoor seating, allowing you to dine al fresco and soak in the vibrant atmosphere of the village. It's a great place for people-watching and enjoying the Florida weather.

Art and Decor: Some shops in Hyde Park Village focus on art, home decor, and interior design, making it a great place to browse for unique pieces to enhance your living space.

Specialty Stores: You can discover specialty stores catering to specific interests, such as wellness, beauty, fashion accessories, and more.

Events and Entertainment: The village often hosts events, promotions, and live entertainment. Check their event calendar for any scheduled activities during your visit.

Historic Charm: Hyde Park Village retains its historic charm with brick-paved streets, tree-lined sidewalks, and historic architecture. Strolling through the village is a pleasant experience in itself.

Pet-Friendly: The district is often pet-friendly, and you may find water bowls and designated areas for your furry friends.

Parking: Convenient parking is typically available, including street parking and parking garages, making it easy to explore the area.

Local Community: The village is a popular gathering spot for the local community, offering a sense of camaraderie and a place to connect with neighbors and friends.

Holiday Decor: During the holiday season, the village is often beautifully decorated with festive lights and decorations, creating a festive atmosphere.

Hours of Operation: Be sure to check the official Hyde Park Village website or contact individual stores and restaurants for their specific hours of operation.

Hyde Park Village provides a delightful shopping and dining experience, blending modern retail with historic charm. Whether you're looking for the perfect gift, enjoying a leisurely meal, or simply exploring the picturesque surroundings, the village offers a welcoming and upscale environment for residents and visitors alike.

85.Go on a Tampa Bay ghost hunting tour.

Embarking on a Tampa Bay ghost hunting tour is a spine-tingling and immersive experience for those intrigued by the supernatural, local legends, and haunted history. These tours take participants to locations with reported paranormal activity and provide an opportunity to explore the eerie side of Tampa Bay. Here's what you can typically expect when going on a ghost hunting tour in the Tampa Bay area:

Experienced Guides: Knowledgeable guides lead the tour and share chilling stories, historical facts, and paranormal accounts associated with the locations you'll visit.

Haunted Sites: The tour typically takes you to haunted locations, such as old buildings, cemeteries, historic districts, or areas with a history of reported ghostly activity.

History and Legends: Guides often provide historical context and share local legends and folklore related to the haunted sites. You'll learn about the mysterious events and the people who once lived there.

Ghost Hunting Equipment: Some tours provide participants with ghost hunting equipment, such as EMF meters, dowsing rods, or spirit communication devices, to use during the tour.

EVP Sessions: Electronic Voice Phenomenon (EVP) sessions may be part of the tour, allowing participants to attempt to communicate with spirits using recording devices.

Photography and Documentation: Ghost hunters are encouraged to take photographs and document their experiences during the tour. Some claim to capture orbs or unexplained phenomena in their pictures.

Stories and Encounters: Guides often share stories of reported ghostly encounters, sightings, and personal experiences from previous tours.

Interactive: Depending on the tour, you may have opportunities to engage in interactive paranormal investigations, such as conducting spirit communication sessions or attempting to capture EVPs.

Nighttime Tours: Many ghost hunting tours take place at night, creating a spooky atmosphere that enhances the experience.

Group Size: The size of the tour group can vary, so check with the tour operator for information on group sizes and reservations.

Safety Measures: While these tours are meant to be spooky and entertaining, safety is a priority. Guides typically provide safety instructions and ensure that participants do not enter restricted or unsafe areas.

Duration: The length of the tour can vary, so be sure to check the tour's official website or contact the operator for details on the duration and meeting points.

Ghost hunting tours offer an opportunity to explore the unknown and test your courage as you venture into the realm of the paranormal. Whether you're a believer in the supernatural or simply looking for a unique and eerie experience, a Tampa Bay ghost hunting tour can be a thrilling adventure into the mysteries of the afterlife. Keep in mind that these tours are primarily for entertainment and should be enjoyed with an open mind and a sense of curiosity.

86. Visit the Tampa Port Authority.

The Tampa Port Authority, officially known as the Tampa Port Authority - Port Tampa Bay, is a significant maritime organization responsible for managing and overseeing the seaport facilities in the Tampa Bay area. While it primarily serves as an administrative and operational entity for the port, there are several ways to learn about its activities and impact on the region:

Visitor Center: The Tampa Port Authority may have a visitor center or information center at its headquarters or within the port complex. Here, you can typically find brochures, exhibits, and displays that provide information about the port's history, operations, and economic contributions to the Tampa Bay region.

Guided Tours: Some ports, including Port Tampa Bay, offer guided tours of their facilities. These tours provide insight into the various operations at the port, including cargo handling, container shipping, cruise terminals, and more. They often include commentary on the history and significance of the port.

Educational Programs: Port authorities occasionally offer educational programs and workshops for schools and community groups. These programs can provide a deeper understanding of the maritime industry, trade, and the environment.

Online Resources: The Tampa Port Authority typically maintains an official website with a wealth of information about the port's activities, statistics, news, and community engagement efforts. You can explore their website to learn more about their role in the Tampa Bay area.

Community Engagement: Port authorities often engage with the local community through public meetings, outreach events, and partnerships with local organizations. This can be an opportunity to attend meetings or events to learn about the port's initiatives and community involvement.

Economic Impact: The Tampa Port Authority plays a vital role in the region's economy. You can find reports and studies on their website detailing the economic impact of the port, including job creation, trade, and economic development.

Environmental Stewardship: Ports are increasingly focused on environmental sustainability. The Tampa Port Authority may have initiatives and projects related to environmental stewardship, which you can learn about through their publications and website.

Contact Information: If you have specific questions or would like to learn more about the Tampa Port Authority, you can often contact them directly through their website or by reaching out to their public affairs or communications department.

Visiting the Tampa Port Authority can provide valuable insights into the maritime industry's role in the region, the significance of the port for trade and commerce, and its contributions to the local economy. Whether you're interested in the logistics of cargo handling or the impact of the cruise industry, exploring the activities of the port can be an educational and informative experience. Be sure to check the official Tampa Port Authority website or contact them for the most up-to-date information on visitor opportunities and tours.

87.Attend the Tampa International Fringe Festival.

Attending the Tampa International Fringe Festival is a fantastic way to immerse yourself in a diverse and exciting world of performing arts. The fringe festival format showcases a wide range of theatrical performances, including plays, comedy, dance, and experimental works, often by emerging or independent artists. Here's what you can typically expect when attending the Tampa International Fringe Festival:

Diverse Performances: The festival features a variety of performances across different genres, from traditional plays to avant-garde experimental theater, circus acts, puppetry, dance, stand-up comedy, and more.

Independent Artists: The fringe festival often provides a platform for emerging and independent artists to showcase their work. You may have the opportunity to discover new talent and innovative performances.

Venues: Festival performances typically take place in multiple venues throughout the city, including theaters, galleries, and unconventional spaces. Each venue offers a unique atmosphere and setting for the shows.

Fringe Atmosphere: The fringe festival has a lively and inclusive atmosphere, encouraging artistic experimentation and pushing boundaries. It's a place where artists can take creative risks.

Accessibility: Shows are usually affordable and accessible, making it possible to attend multiple performances during the festival.

International Flavor: While it's called the Tampa International Fringe Festival, you can often expect a mix of local, national, and international performers, creating a diverse and culturally rich experience.

Interactive Experiences: Some fringe performances may involve audience participation, blurring the lines between the performers and the audience.

Artistic Exchange: The festival often promotes dialogue between artists and audiences, providing opportunities for post-show discussions, Q&A sessions, and feedback.

Community Engagement: Fringe festivals often engage with the local community through workshops, educational programs, and outreach activities.

Food and Socializing: Some fringe festivals include food vendors, social spaces, and opportunities for networking and mingling with artists and fellow festivalgoers.

Festival Passes: Depending on the festival's format, you may have the option to purchase festival passes that grant access to multiple shows at a discounted rate.

Online Resources: Check the festival's official website or program for show schedules, venue details, ticket information, and any special events or promotions.

The Tampa International Fringe Festival is an exciting cultural event that celebrates the performing arts in all their forms. Whether you're a theater enthusiast, an art lover, or simply looking for a unique and thought-provoking experience, attending the fringe festival can be a rewarding and entertaining adventure. Be sure to check the festival's official website for the most up-to-date information on show listings, schedules, and ticketing details.

88.Explore Ballast Point Park.

Ballast Point Park is a picturesque waterfront park located in the Ballast Point neighborhood of Tampa, Florida. Offering stunning views of Tampa Bay, this park provides a peaceful and scenic environment for residents and visitors to enjoy. Here's what you can typically expect when exploring Ballast Point Park:

Waterfront Views: The park is known for its panoramic views of Tampa Bay, making it an ideal spot to watch sailboats, cruise ships, and wildlife. The park's fishing pier extends into the bay, allowing anglers to cast their lines while taking in the beautiful surroundings.

Picnic Areas: Ballast Point Park features picnic areas with tables and grills. It's a popular spot for picnicking with family and friends, enjoying a meal with a view of the bay.

Playground: The park has a playground area where children can enjoy swings, slides, and other play equipment. It's a great place for families to spend quality time together.

Travel to Tampa Florida

Fitness Trail: There's a fitness trail that winds through the park, providing opportunities for walking, jogging, or running. It's a scenic route for those looking to stay active while enjoying the outdoors.

Boat Ramp: A public boat ramp is available for boaters to launch their vessels into Tampa Bay, making it convenient for those who want to explore the bay by boat.

Gardens: Ballast Point Park is adorned with lush landscaping and well-maintained gardens, offering a peaceful and aesthetically pleasing environment for visitors.

Fishing: Whether you're an experienced angler or just enjoy casting a line, the park's fishing pier is a great place to try your luck at catching fish.

Events and Gatherings: The park occasionally hosts community events, festivals, and gatherings, so be sure to check the local event calendar for any happenings during your visit.

Wildlife Viewing: Keep an eye out for the diverse range of wildlife that inhabits the area, including birds, dolphins, and the occasional manatee.

Sunsets: Ballast Point Park is a popular spot to watch the sunset over Tampa Bay. The unobstructed views provide a stunning backdrop for evening relaxation.

Dog-Friendly: The park is often pet-friendly, allowing leashed dogs to accompany their owners on walks and enjoy the outdoors.

Historical Significance: The park's name is derived from its historical role as a ballast point for ships. Interpretive signage may provide insights into the park's history.

Accessibility: The park is typically accessible to people with mobility challenges, with accessible pathways and facilities.

Ballast Point Park offers a serene escape from the bustle of city life and is a popular spot for both locals and visitors to unwind, enjoy the outdoors, and savor the natural beauty of Tampa Bay. Whether you're interested in a leisurely picnic, a scenic walk, or simply taking in the tranquil views, the park provides a peaceful oasis by the water.

89.Go on a Tampa Bay fishing charter.

Going on a Tampa Bay fishing charter is an exciting adventure for both experienced anglers and those new to fishing. Tampa Bay offers a diverse and thriving ecosystem, making it a prime destination for fishing enthusiasts. Here's what you can typically expect when booking a fishing charter in Tampa Bay:

Variety of Fish: Tampa Bay is home to a wide variety of fish species, including snook, redfish, trout, tarpon, grouper, snapper, and more. The type of fish you target will often depend on the season and your preferences.

Experienced Guides: Fishing charters are typically led by experienced and knowledgeable captains who know the local waters and can provide guidance on the best fishing spots, techniques, and bait.

All-Inclusive Equipment: Most fishing charters provide all the necessary fishing equipment, including rods, reels, bait, and tackle. You won't need to bring your own gear.

Boat Types: Charters may offer different types of boats, such as flats boats, bay boats, or offshore vessels, depending on the type of fishing experience you desire.

Customized Trips: Fishing charters can often be customized to your preferences. Whether you want a half-day trip, a full-day excursion, or a specific fishing experience (e.g., fly fishing or deep-sea fishing), you can often find a charter that suits your needs.

Fishing Licenses: Many charters include fishing licenses for their guests, so you won't need to worry about obtaining one separately.

Scenic Views: Tampa Bay's waters provide beautiful views of the bay, mangroves, and the surrounding coastline, offering a picturesque backdrop for your fishing adventure.

Wildlife Watching: While fishing, you might have the chance to observe local wildlife, such as dolphins, manatees, seabirds, and more.

Clean and Well-Maintained Boats: Charter boats are typically well-maintained and equipped with safety gear to ensure a safe and enjoyable experience.

Expertise: Your captain and crew are often experts not only in fishing but also in the natural history of the area, providing interesting insights about the local ecosystem.

Cleaning and Packaging: Some charters offer services to clean and package the fish you catch, making it easy to take your fresh catch home for a meal.

Group Size: Fishing charters can accommodate different group sizes, from solo anglers to larger parties. Be sure to book a charter that fits your group's needs.

Reservations: It's advisable to make reservations in advance, especially during peak fishing seasons, to secure your spot on a preferred charter.

Tampa Bay fishing charters offer an opportunity to experience the thrill of fishing in a diverse and vibrant aquatic environment. Whether you're seeking a leisurely day on the water, a chance to catch trophy fish, or simply want to enjoy the outdoors, a fishing charter in Tampa Bay provides an unforgettable experience. Be sure to communicate your goals and preferences with the charter captain to ensure a tailored and enjoyable fishing trip.

90. Visit the Tampa Bay Estuary Program.

The Tampa Bay Estuary Program (TBEP) is a vital organization dedicated to the preservation and restoration of Tampa Bay's delicate ecosystem. While the TBEP primarily focuses on environmental conservation and research, there are ways for interested individuals to learn more about their work and the importance of preserving the estuary:

Educational Programs: The TBEP often offers educational programs, workshops, and seminars related to the ecology and conservation of the Tampa Bay estuary. These programs can be informative and engaging for those interested in environmental science and conservation.

Publications: The program may produce publications, reports, and educational materials that provide insights into the health of Tampa Bay and the efforts being made to protect it. These materials may be available online or through local educational institutions.

Community Outreach: The TBEP frequently engages with the local community through outreach events, such as environmental fairs, clean-up initiatives, and volunteer opportunities. Participating in these events can provide hands-on experience and a deeper understanding of estuary conservation.

Guided Tours: Some estuary programs offer guided tours of estuarine habitats and restoration sites. These tours may be available on boats or as walking tours, allowing participants to see the beauty and complexity of the estuary up close.

Visitor Center: The TBEP may have a visitor center or information center where you can learn about the estuary's ecology, conservation efforts, and local wildlife. Interactive exhibits and displays are often available for visitors.

Volunteer Opportunities: Many estuary programs rely on volunteers to assist with conservation and restoration efforts. Volunteering is a hands-on way to contribute to the health of the estuary while learning about its importance.

Public Meetings: Estuary programs often hold public meetings and workshops where community members can learn about ongoing projects, ask questions, and provide input on environmental initiatives.

Online Resources: The TBEP typically maintains an official website with a wealth of information on the estuary, including research findings, conservation projects, and educational resources.

Partnerships: The TBEP often collaborates with other local, state, and federal agencies, as well as nonprofit organizations, to achieve its conservation goals. Exploring these partnerships can provide additional opportunities for involvement.

Research Opportunities: If you're a student or researcher interested in studying estuarine ecology, the TBEP may have information on research projects and opportunities to collaborate.

Visiting or engaging with the Tampa Bay Estuary Program can be a rewarding experience for those interested in environmental conservation and the protection of natural ecosystems. Learning about the delicate balance of life within the estuary, the challenges it faces, and the efforts being made to ensure its health is both educational and inspiring. Be sure to check the TBEP's official website or contact them directly for the most up-to-date information on educational programs, events, and volunteer opportunities.

91.Attend the Tampa Bay Comic Con.

Attending the Tampa Bay Comic Con is an exciting experience for fans of comics, pop culture, science fiction, fantasy, and all things geek and nerd. This annual event typically features a wide range of activities, guest appearances, vendors, and opportunities for fans to immerse themselves in the world of comics and entertainment. Here's what you can typically expect when attending the Tampa Bay Comic Con:

Celebrity Guests: The convention often invites celebrity guests from various entertainment genres, including actors, artists, authors, and creators. Attendees can have the opportunity to meet their favorite stars, get autographs, and take photos with them.

Artist Alley: Artist Alley is a popular section of the convention where comic book artists, writers, and illustrators showcase their work, sign comics, and interact with fans. It's a great place to discover new talent and collect unique artwork.

Cosplay: Cosplay (costume play) is a significant part of the convention. Many attendees come dressed as their favorite characters from comics, movies, video games, and TV shows. There are often cosplay contests and photo opportunities for participants and fans.

Vendor Hall: The vendor hall is filled with exhibitors offering a wide array of merchandise, including comic books, collectibles, toys, clothing, artwork, and more. It's a shopping paradise for collectors and fans.

Panels and Workshops: The convention typically hosts panels and workshops on a variety of topics, including comic book creation, pop culture discussions, and behind-the-scenes insights from industry professionals.

Gaming: Gaming enthusiasts can enjoy tabletop gaming, video game tournaments, and interactive experiences related to their favorite games.

Kids' Zone: Many conventions have a dedicated Kids' Zone with family-friendly activities, workshops, and entertainment to engage younger attendees.

Photo Opportunities: Throughout the convention, you'll find themed photo opportunities, backdrops, and props to capture memorable moments with friends and cosplayers.

Autograph Sessions: Besides meeting celebrities, attendees can often attend autograph sessions and purchase memorabilia signed by their favorite artists and actors.

Themed Events: Some conventions host themed events, parties, and gatherings in the evenings, offering additional opportunities for socializing and fun.

Fan Communities: Tampa Bay Comic Con is a great place to connect with fellow fans who share your interests and passions. You can join discussions, make new friends, and bond over your love of comics and pop culture.

Tickets and Passes: Tickets to the convention are typically available for single days or the entire weekend, with options for VIP experiences or early access. Be sure to check the official Tampa Bay Comic Con website for ticketing information and pricing.

The Tampa Bay Comic Con is an excellent opportunity to celebrate your favorite fandoms, meet like-minded individuals, and enjoy a weekend filled with entertainment and creativity. Whether you're a long-time comic book collector, a cosplayer, or simply looking for a fun and immersive experience, this convention offers something for everyone in the world of geek culture. Be sure to check the official convention website for the latest updates on guest appearances, schedules, and special events.

92.Explore the Westchase Golf Club.

The Westchase Golf Club is a popular golfing destination located in the Westchase community of Tampa, Florida. Known for its well-maintained course and picturesque surroundings, the golf club offers a great experience for both avid golfers and those looking to enjoy a day on the links. Here's what you can typically expect when exploring the Westchase Golf Club:

Championship Golf Course: The Westchase Golf Club features an 18-hole, par-72 championship golf course designed by renowned architect Lloyd Clifton. The course is known for its challenging layout, beautiful landscaping, and a variety of water hazards and bunkers.

Practice Facilities: The golf club often provides practice facilities, including a driving range, putting green, and chipping area. These facilities are perfect for warming up before your round or working on your swing.

Pro Shop: The pro shop offers a selection of golf equipment, apparel, accessories, and golf balls. It's a convenient place to stock up on any golfing essentials.

Golf Lessons: If you're new to golf or looking to improve your skills, the Westchase Golf Club may offer golf lessons with experienced instructors. Private and group lessons are typically available.

Golf Tournaments: The club may host various golf tournaments and events throughout the year. These events can be a fun way to test your skills and compete with other golfers.

Clubhouse: The clubhouse is a hub for golfers to relax before or after their rounds. It often includes a restaurant or grill where you can enjoy a meal or refreshments.

Scenic Views: The course is usually set amidst lush Florida landscapes with native vegetation, water features, and well-maintained fairways and greens. It provides a serene and picturesque backdrop for your golfing experience.

Membership Options: The golf club may offer various membership options, including annual memberships, seasonal memberships, and more. These memberships often come with benefits such as reduced greens fees and priority tee times.

Golf Carts: Golf carts are typically available for rent, making it convenient to navigate the course and transport your clubs.

Tee Time Reservations: It's advisable to make tee time reservations in advance, especially during peak golfing seasons, to secure your preferred playing time.

Golf Etiquette: Familiarize yourself with golf etiquette and course rules to ensure an enjoyable and respectful experience for yourself and fellow golfers.

The Westchase Golf Club provides a serene and challenging golfing experience in the Tampa Bay area. Whether you're a serious golfer looking to test your skills or a casual player seeking a relaxing round of golf, the club offers a well-maintained course and excellent amenities for a day on the links. Be sure to check the club's official website or contact them directly for the latest information on tee times, rates, and any special events or promotions.

93.Go on a paddleboard yoga session.

Participating in a paddleboard yoga session combines the physical and mental benefits of yoga with the serenity of being on the water. In Tampa Bay, with its beautiful waterways and warm climate, paddleboard yoga is a popular activity. Here's what you can typically expect when going on a paddleboard yoga session:

Location: Paddleboard yoga sessions are usually held in calm and shallow water bodies, such as bays, lakes, or calm sections of rivers. In Tampa Bay, you may find sessions in various locations, including beaches, marinas, and designated paddleboarding areas.

Equipment: Paddleboard yoga sessions typically include all necessary equipment, such as a paddleboard, paddle, and a secure anchor system to keep the board stable during the practice. Some sessions may also provide personal flotation devices (PFDs) for safety.

Instructor: A certified paddleboard yoga instructor leads the session. They are experienced in both yoga and paddleboarding and guide participants through the practice.

Basic Paddleboarding Instruction: If you're new to paddleboarding, the instructor often provides a brief tutorial on paddling techniques and balancing on the board before the yoga session begins.

Yoga Practice: The yoga session itself includes a series of yoga poses and stretches adapted for the paddleboard. Poses are often chosen for their suitability on the water, with an emphasis on balance and stability. Expect a mix of traditional yoga poses and variations designed for the paddleboard.

Mindfulness and Connection: Paddleboard yoga encourages mindfulness, as the gentle movement of the water and the sounds of nature create a unique and peaceful environment. Participants are often encouraged to connect with the natural surroundings and focus on their breath.

Challenge and Balance: Paddleboard yoga adds an extra layer of challenge to your yoga practice due to the instability of the board. It requires greater engagement of your core muscles and heightened awareness of your body's balance.

Cool-Down and Relaxation: The session typically concludes with a cool-down and relaxation period, allowing participants to lie on their backs on the paddleboard and drift while taking in the tranquil surroundings.

All Levels Welcome: Paddleboard yoga sessions are usually suitable for all levels of yoga practitioners, from beginners to experienced yogis. The instructor may offer modifications to make poses accessible to everyone.

Water Fun: After the yoga practice, some sessions allow participants to enjoy paddling around or even taking a swim if conditions permit.

Safety: Safety is a priority, and participants are often required to wear a PFD or leash, especially in open water settings. The instructor provides guidance on water safety.

Reservations: It's advisable to make reservations in advance, especially during peak seasons, to secure your spot in the session.

Paddleboard yoga offers a unique and peaceful way to connect with nature, enhance your yoga practice, and enjoy the serene waters of Tampa Bay. It's a great way to experience mindfulness, balance, and relaxation while staying active and enjoying the beauty of the outdoors. Check with local paddleboard yoga providers in the Tampa Bay area for session availability, schedules, and any specific requirements or recommendations.

94. Visit the Tampa Bay Performing Arts Center.

The Tampa Bay Performing Arts Center, commonly known as the Straz Center for the Performing Arts, is a prominent cultural institution located in downtown Tampa, Florida. This world-class venue serves as a hub for various performing arts, including theater, music, dance, and more. Here's what you can typically expect when visiting the Tampa Bay Performing Arts Center:

Theater Productions: The Straz Center hosts a diverse range of theater productions, including Broadway shows, musicals, dramas, and comedy performances. Check the center's schedule for upcoming productions and ticket availability.

Concerts: The center often hosts concerts featuring various genres of music, from classical to contemporary. You may have the opportunity to see orchestras, chamber ensembles, soloists, bands, and vocalists perform in one of the center's concert halls.

Dance Performances: Dance companies from around the world frequently grace the Straz Center's stages, offering ballet, modern dance, contemporary dance, and other dance forms.

Opera and Classical Music: Enjoy operatic performances and classical music concerts by acclaimed artists and ensembles.

Children's Programming: The center often provides family-friendly programming, including children's theater productions, educational workshops, and interactive performances designed for young audiences.

Educational Programs: Look for educational and outreach programs, including student matinees, workshops, and lecture series, aimed at promoting arts education and engagement.

Multiple Venues: The Straz Center boasts multiple performance venues, such as the Carol Morsani Hall, Ferguson Hall, Jaeb Theater, and TECO Theater. Each venue offers a unique atmosphere and accommodates various types of performances.

Art Galleries: Explore art galleries within the Straz Center that often feature rotating exhibitions of visual art.

Dining and Refreshments: The center may have on-site dining options and bars where you can enjoy pre-show meals or drinks.

Accessibility: The Straz Center typically provides accessibility services, including wheelchair access, assistive listening devices, and sign language interpretation upon request.

Ticketing: Purchase tickets in advance online, by phone, or at the box office. Depending on the performance, ticket availability may vary, so it's recommended to plan ahead.

Parking: The center offers convenient parking options, including garages and surface lots, for visitors attending events.

Cultural Events: Keep an eye on the center's calendar for special cultural events, festivals, and collaborations with local arts organizations.

Gift Shop: The center often features a gift shop where you can purchase souvenirs, books, and merchandise related to the performing arts.

Lobby and Common Areas: Enjoy the beautiful lobby and common areas, which may include artwork, sculptures, and spaces to relax before and after performances.

The Straz Center for the Performing Arts is a cultural gem in the Tampa Bay area, offering a rich array of performing arts experiences for residents and visitors alike. Whether you're interested in enjoying a world-class theater production, listening to live music, or immersing yourself in dance and the arts, the Straz Center provides a vibrant and enriching cultural experience. Be sure to visit the center's official website for the most up-to-date information on upcoming performances, ticketing, and special events.

95.Attend a Tampa Bay Roller Derby match.

Attending a Tampa Bay Roller Derby match is a thrilling and action-packed experience that combines athleticism, strategy, and community spirit. Roller derby is a fast-paced, full-contact sport that has gained popularity for its exciting bouts and passionate fan base. Here's what you can typically expect when attending a Tampa Bay Roller Derby match:

Venue: Tampa Bay Roller Derby matches are often held at local roller rinks or dedicated roller derby venues. These venues provide a unique and intimate setting for fans to get up close to the action.

Teams: Tampa Bay Roller Derby typically features multiple teams, each with its own unique name and identity. Teams may compete against each other in various bouts or matches.

Bouts: Roller derby bouts consist of two teams competing against each other on a flat track. Each bout is divided into two halves, and each half is further divided into jams, which are short periods of play.

Skaters: Roller derby skaters, often referred to as "derby girls" or "derby athletes," compete on roller skates and are known for their speed, agility, and physicality. Skaters play various roles on the track, including jammers and blockers.

Rules: Roller derby has specific rules and scoring systems. Jammers attempt to score points by lapping members of the opposing team, while blockers aim to stop the opposing jammer and assist their own jammer.

Action: Roller derby is a full-contact sport, and the bouts are known for their fast-paced action, strategic gameplay, and hard hits. It's common to see skaters making strategic passes, executing body checks, and maneuvering through the pack.

Fan Engagement: Roller derby matches often have enthusiastic and engaged fans who cheer for their favorite teams and skaters. Attendees are encouraged to get into the spirit and support their local derby community.

Halftime Entertainment: During halftime, there may be entertainment, activities, or performances to keep the audience engaged and entertained.

Merchandise and Souvenirs: Roller derby events often have merchandise booths where you can purchase team gear, apparel, and souvenirs.

Family-Friendly: Roller derby is typically family-friendly, and many events welcome fans of all ages. Some leagues even have junior roller derby programs for kids.

Community Involvement: Roller derby leagues often have a strong sense of community involvement, with skaters and fans supporting local charities and causes.

Meet and Greet: After the bout, there's often a chance to meet the skaters, take photos, and learn more about roller derby.

Attending a Tampa Bay Roller Derby match is not only an exciting sports experience but also an opportunity to support a vibrant and dedicated local community. Whether you're a seasoned roller derby fan or new to the sport, the matches are sure to provide an adrenaline-filled and entertaining day out. Be sure to check the official Tampa Bay Roller Derby website or social media channels for information on upcoming matches, ticketing, and any special events or promotions.

96.Explore the Veterans Memorial Park and Museum.

Veterans Memorial Park and Museum is a significant cultural and historical destination in the Tampa Bay area dedicated to honoring the contributions and sacrifices of veterans. Located in the heart of Tampa, Florida, the park and museum offer a unique opportunity to learn about military history, pay tribute to veterans, and reflect on the nation's military heritage. Here's what you can typically expect when exploring Veterans Memorial Park and Museum:

Outdoor Memorial: The park features an outdoor memorial area with various monuments and memorials dedicated to different branches of the military, specific conflicts, and veterans' organizations. These memorials provide a solemn and reflective space to honor and remember veterans.

Reflective Atmosphere: Visitors often find the park to be a peaceful and contemplative environment, making it suitable for quiet reflection and paying respects to veterans.

Educational Exhibits: The museum typically houses a collection of artifacts, exhibits, and displays that highlight the history of the military, the experiences of veterans, and the significance of military service. These exhibits may include uniforms, equipment, photographs, documents, and more.

Veteran Stories: Some museums within the park may feature oral history recordings, interviews, and personal stories from veterans, allowing visitors to gain insight into their experiences and perspectives.

Educational Programs: The museum often offers educational programs, workshops, lectures, and events related to military history and veterans' experiences. These programs can be engaging and informative for visitors of all ages.

Events: Veterans Memorial Park and Museum may host special events throughout the year, such as Memorial Day and Veterans Day ceremonies, which provide opportunities to participate in patriotic observances.

Gift Shop: Many museums have gift shops where visitors can purchase military-themed merchandise, books, and souvenirs.

Guided Tours: Guided tours may be available to provide in-depth insights into the exhibits and memorials within the park and museum.

Accessibility: The park and museum typically prioritize accessibility, with features like ramps, wide walkways, and other accommodations to ensure that all visitors can enjoy the experience.

Honoring Veterans: The primary focus of Veterans Memorial Park and Museum is to honor and remember veterans from all branches of the military, spanning various conflicts and eras.

Community Involvement: The park often collaborates with local veterans' organizations, schools, and community groups to promote awareness and appreciation of veterans' contributions.

Free Admission: Many museums within the park offer free admission to the public, making it an accessible and educational destination for all.

Visiting Veterans Memorial Park and Museum is not only an opportunity to learn about military history but also a chance to express gratitude and pay tribute to the men and women who have served their country. Whether you have a personal connection to the military or simply want to gain a deeper understanding of our nation's history, this destination offers a meaningful and enriching experience. Before your visit, it's a good idea to check the park's official website or contact them directly for the latest information on hours of operation, exhibits, and any special events or programs.

97.Go on a Tampa Bay brewery crawl.

Embarking on a Tampa Bay brewery crawl is a fantastic way to explore the flourishing craft beer scene in the Tampa Bay area. With numerous breweries offering a wide range of unique brews, you can savor different styles, flavors, and atmospheres at each stop. Here's how to plan your brewery crawl:

Start by researching the breweries in the Tampa Bay area. Tampa is known for its craft beer scene, and you'll find a variety of options, from established names to newer, innovative breweries.

Choose a central starting point for your brewery crawl. You can pick a specific neighborhood or area with several breweries close to each other to make transportation easier. Ybor City, Seminole Heights, and the Tampa Heights area are popular choices.

Decide how you'll get from one brewery to another. Options include designated drivers, rideshare services, or even organized brewery tours if available.

Verify the opening and closing times of the breweries you plan to visit. Some breweries may have limited hours or specific days when they're closed.

Consider the availability of food at each brewery. Some breweries have on-site restaurants or food trucks, while others might have limited food options. Plan accordingly if you want to enjoy meals along with your beer.

Many breweries offer sample flights, which allow you to taste a variety of their beers. It's an excellent way to explore different styles and flavors without committing to a full pint.

Bring a notebook or use a smartphone app to take notes on the beers you try. This can help you remember your favorites for future reference.

If you're curious about the brewing process or want to learn more about the beers, don't hesitate to strike up a conversation with the brewmasters or staff. They're often passionate about their craft and eager to share their knowledge.

Part of the brewery experience is soaking in the atmosphere. Take your time at each brewery, enjoy the decor, and relax with friends or fellow beer enthusiasts.

- Always drink responsibly and know your limits. It's essential to have a designated driver or alternative transportation arranged if you plan to sample multiple beers.

- Some breweries may have merchandise for sale, such as branded glassware, shirts, or hats. Consider collecting souvenirs to commemorate your brewery crawl.

- Drinking water between beer samples can help you stay hydrated and pace yourself throughout the crawl.

- If you're walking between breweries, be mindful of traffic and pedestrian safety, especially if you're in an area with heavy traffic.

Tampa Bay's craft beer scene offers a wide array of flavors and experiences, making it an excellent destination for a brewery crawl. Whether you're a seasoned beer aficionado or just looking for a fun and flavorful outing with friends, exploring the local breweries in Tampa Bay can be a memorable and enjoyable experience.

98. Visit the Tampa Bay Downs Golf Practice Facility.

The Tampa Bay Downs Golf Practice Facility is a fantastic destination for golf enthusiasts looking to improve their skills or simply enjoy a day of practice and recreation. Located in Tampa, Florida, this facility offers a range of amenities to help golfers of all levels hone their game. Here's what you can typically expect when visiting the Tampa Bay Downs Golf Practice Facility:

Driving Range: The facility often features a spacious driving range with multiple hitting bays. Golfers can practice their drives, iron shots, and short game in a controlled environment. The driving range usually provides both grass and mat tees to accommodate different preferences.

Practice Greens: In addition to the driving range, there are typically putting greens and chipping areas where golfers can work on their putting and short game skills. These greens often mimic the conditions found on actual golf courses.

Golf Instructors: Some practice facilities offer professional golf instructors who can provide lessons and personalized coaching to help golfers improve their techniques. Lessons are often available for golfers of all skill levels, from beginners to advanced players.

Club Fitting: The facility may offer club fitting services, allowing golfers to assess and optimize their club selections to suit their individual swing characteristics and preferences.

Equipment Rental: Golf clubs and other equipment may be available for rent for those who don't have their own gear.

Golf Balls: Typically, the facility provides golf balls for practice at the driving range. You can purchase a bucket of balls to use during your practice session.

Scenic Setting: Many practice facilities are set in a picturesque environment, providing a serene and enjoyable backdrop for your golf practice.

Covered Areas: Some facilities have covered or shaded hitting bays, allowing golfers to practice even in inclement weather or during hot Florida summers.

Open to the Public: Golf practice facilities like Tampa Bay Downs are often open to the public, so you don't need a membership to use the amenities.

Affordable Rates: Practice facility fees are generally reasonable, making it an accessible option for golfers looking to refine their skills without committing to a full round of golf.

Hours of Operation: Check the facility's hours of operation, as they may vary seasonally or due to special events.

Pro Shop: Some practice facilities have a pro shop where you can purchase golf equipment, accessories, and attire.

Visiting the Tampa Bay Downs Golf Practice Facility is an excellent way to work on your golf game, whether you're a beginner looking to learn the basics or an experienced golfer striving to perfect your swing. It provides a comfortable and supportive environment for golfers to practice and refine their skills. Before heading to the facility, consider checking their official website or contacting them directly for information on operating hours, rates, and any special services they may offer.

99.Attend the Gasparilla International Film Festival.

The Gasparilla International Film Festival is a highly anticipated annual event in Tampa, Florida, that celebrates the art of filmmaking by showcasing a diverse selection of independent films from around the world. This festival provides a unique opportunity for film enthusiasts, industry professionals, and the local community to come together and enjoy a wide range of cinematic creations. Here's what you can typically expect when attending the Gasparilla International Film Festival:

Film Screenings: The heart of the festival is the screening of a variety of films, including feature-length narratives, documentaries, short films, and experimental works. These films often represent different genres, styles, and cultural perspectives.

World Premieres: Some films featured in the festival are world premieres, providing attendees with the chance to be among the first to see groundbreaking cinematic works.

Q&A Sessions: After select screenings, filmmakers, directors, actors, and crew members often participate in question-and-answer sessions, allowing the audience to gain insights into the creative process and the stories behind the films.

Awards and Competitions: Many film festivals, including Gasparilla, host awards ceremonies to recognize outstanding contributions to cinema. Awards may include categories like Best Feature, Best Documentary, Best Director, and Audience Choice.

Networking Opportunities: The festival often attracts filmmakers, producers, distributors, and other industry professionals. Attendees can network with these individuals, fostering connections and opportunities within the world of film.

Workshops and Panels: The festival may offer educational workshops, panels, and discussions on various aspects of filmmaking, from screenwriting and directing to producing and film financing.

Cultural Exchange: Gasparilla International Film Festival often features films from diverse backgrounds, fostering cultural exchange and promoting a global perspective on cinema.

Parties and Social Events: Film festivals often host parties, receptions, and social events where attendees can relax, socialize, and discuss the films they've seen.

Venue: The festival typically takes place at various venues throughout Tampa, including theaters, cultural centers, and other film-related spaces.

Tickets: Tickets are usually available for individual screenings, festival passes, or VIP packages, allowing attendees to customize their festival experience.

Local Flavor: Gasparilla International Film Festival often showcases films created by local filmmakers or featuring stories related to the Tampa Bay area.

Film Market: Some festivals include a film market where industry professionals can explore distribution opportunities for selected films.

Community Engagement: Beyond the screenings and events, the festival may also engage with the local community through outreach programs, film education initiatives, and collaborations with local organizations.

The Gasparilla International Film Festival is not only a platform for film appreciation but also a dynamic cultural event that promotes the art of storytelling through cinema. Whether you're a passionate cinephile or someone curious about independent filmmaking, attending this festival offers a unique opportunity to immerse yourself in the world of cinema, discover new voices and perspectives, and engage with the vibrant film community in Tampa. Be sure to check the festival's official website for the most up-to-date information on dates, film selections, ticketing, and special events.

100.Explore the Upper Tampa Bay Conservation Park.

Upper Tampa Bay Conservation Park is a beautiful natural oasis located in Tampa, Florida, offering visitors a chance to explore the area's unique ecosystems and wildlife. This conservation park provides a range of outdoor activities and opportunities to connect with nature. Here's what you can typically expect when exploring the Upper Tampa Bay Conservation Park:

Hiking Trails: The park features a network of well-maintained hiking trails that wind through various natural habitats, including pine flatwoods, hardwood hammocks, and saltwater marshes. These trails are suitable for hikers of all levels and offer scenic views of the surrounding environment.

Wildlife Viewing: Birdwatchers and wildlife enthusiasts will appreciate the park's diverse fauna. It's a haven for birdwatching, and you may spot various species of birds, including herons, egrets, ospreys, and possibly even bald eagles. Keep an eye out for turtles, alligators, and other wildlife as well.

Boardwalks and Observation Decks: The park features boardwalks and observation decks that extend over the saltwater marshes. These vantage points provide an up-close look at the unique estuarine ecosystem and its inhabitants.

Picnicking: Picnic areas with tables and shelters are available, making it an ideal spot for a family picnic or a leisurely lunch amid nature.

Canoeing and Kayaking: The park offers opportunities for paddling in the estuarine waters of Tampa Bay. Bring your own canoe or kayak, or check if rentals are available nearby.

Fishing: Fishing is permitted in designated areas, and anglers can try their luck at catching a variety of fish species found in the bay.

Education and Interpretive Programs: Some conservation parks provide educational programs, guided hikes, and interpretive displays to help visitors learn about the park's natural history, ecosystems, and conservation efforts.

Photography: The park's picturesque landscapes, wildlife, and diverse plant life make it a popular destination for photographers and nature enthusiasts.

Geocaching: Geocaching enthusiasts can search for hidden caches within the park, adding an element of treasure hunting to their outdoor adventure.

Visitor Center: Some conservation parks have visitor centers where you can obtain maps, information, and resources about the park's natural features and activities.

Dog-Friendly: Check the park's rules and regulations, as some conservation areas may allow leashed dogs on designated trails.

Environmental Stewardship: Conservation parks like Upper Tampa Bay often play a crucial role in protecting and preserving delicate ecosystems. Be mindful of Leave No Trace principles and respect the park's rules to help safeguard its natural beauty.

Before visiting the Upper Tampa Bay Conservation Park, it's a good idea to check the park's official website or contact them directly to confirm the latest information on hours of operation, trail conditions, rules, and any special programs or events. Whether you're interested in hiking, birdwatching, or simply enjoying a peaceful day in nature, this conservation park offers a serene and educational escape from the hustle and bustle of city life in Tampa.

101.Go on a guided bike tour of Tampa.

Going on a guided bike tour of Tampa is an excellent way to explore the city's diverse neighborhoods, iconic landmarks, and scenic waterfront areas while enjoying a leisurely ride. These tours are typically led by knowledgeable guides who provide insights into the city's history, culture, and local attractions. Here's what you can generally expect on a guided bike tour of Tampa:

Bike Rental: Most guided tours provide participants with a well-maintained bicycle, helmet, and any necessary safety equipment. You can choose from various types of bikes, including cruisers, hybrids, or electric bikes, depending on your preference and fitness level.

Experienced Guides: Knowledgeable and friendly guides lead the tours. They often share interesting facts, historical anecdotes, and insider tips about the city as you ride along.

Scenic Routes: Tours typically follow scenic routes that showcase Tampa's top attractions, parks, and waterfront areas. Common stops may include downtown Tampa, the Tampa Riverwalk, historic Ybor City, and Bayshore Boulevard.

Landmarks and Points of Interest: Guides point out and provide information about notable landmarks, historic sites, public art installations, and architectural gems along the route.

Cultural Insights: You'll gain insights into Tampa's diverse culture, including its Cuban, Spanish, and Native American influences, as well as its rich maritime history.

Rest Stops: Depending on the tour's duration, there may be scheduled rest stops at local cafes, parks, or attractions, allowing you to take a break, enjoy refreshments, and soak in the atmosphere.

Group Size: Tours typically have a limited number of participants to ensure a personalized and enjoyable experience. Group sizes can vary, so it's a good idea to check with the tour operator.

Safety: Safety is a priority, and guides provide instructions on safe biking practices, including signals, road etiquette, and how to navigate city streets.

Family-Friendly Options: Some bike tours offer family-friendly options, making them suitable for riders of various ages and fitness levels. Child seats or trailers may also be available for families with young children.

Custom Tours: Some tour operators offer customizable options, allowing you to tailor the experience to your interests or special occasions like birthdays or corporate events.

Evening Tours: In addition to daytime tours, some operators offer evening bike tours that showcase Tampa's nightlife, illuminated buildings, and vibrant atmosphere after dark.

Eco-Friendly: Bike tours are an eco-friendly and sustainable way to explore the city, contributing to a greener and healthier environment.

Reservations: It's advisable to make reservations for guided bike tours in advance, especially during peak tourist seasons, to secure your spot.

Before embarking on a guided bike tour of Tampa, check with the tour operator for specific details, including the route, duration, pricing, and any special requirements. Whether you're a local looking to rediscover your city or a visitor eager to explore Tampa's highlights, a guided bike tour offers a fun and informative way to experience the city's vibrant culture and scenic beauty.

102.Visit the Tampa Bay Area Renaissance Festival.

The Tampa Bay Area Renaissance Festival is a beloved annual event that transports visitors back in time to the era of knights, royalty, and medieval merriment. Held in Tampa, Florida, this Renaissance festival offers a lively and immersive experience, complete with period costumes, entertainment, crafts, and food. Here's what you can typically expect when visiting the Tampa Bay Area Renaissance Festival:

Period Costumes: Attendees and festival participants often dress in elaborate Renaissance-era costumes, creating a vibrant and authentic atmosphere reminiscent of a bygone era. Many visitors choose to come in costume, and there are often costume rental or purchase options available on-site.

Themed Village: The festival typically features a themed village that resembles a medieval European market square. You can wander through the village, interact with costumed characters, and explore various artisan shops and stalls.

Entertainment: There's a diverse lineup of entertainment, including jousting tournaments, live music, comedy acts, and street performances. The festival's stages showcase a range of talents, from musicians and magicians to fire eaters and acrobats.

Jousting Tournaments: One of the highlights is the thrilling jousting tournament featuring knights in shining armor. Spectators can cheer on their favorite knights as they compete in mounted combat.

Crafts and Artisans: The festival hosts numerous artisans and craft vendors who sell handmade goods, including jewelry, pottery, leatherwork, clothing, and more. It's an excellent place to find unique and artisanal gifts.

Food and Drink: Feast on a variety of Renaissance-inspired food and drink options, such as turkey legs, mead, roasted nuts, and hearty stews. Vegetarian and gluten-free options are often available.

Interactive Activities: Visitors can participate in various interactive activities, such as archery, axe throwing, and games of skill. These activities add to the festival's interactive and engaging atmosphere.

Children's Activities: The festival is family-friendly, with activities and entertainment geared toward children. There are often puppet shows, storytelling sessions, and kid-friendly games.

Pet-Friendly: Some Renaissance festivals allow attendees to bring their well-behaved pets, often in costume. Check the festival's rules and guidelines regarding pets.

Theme Weekends: Some Renaissance festivals have themed weekends or special events, such as pirate-themed weekends or Celtic celebrations, which add even more variety to the experience.

Educational Demonstrations: Learn about historical crafts and skills through educational demonstrations, such as blacksmithing, weaving, and glassblowing.

Music and Dance: Enjoy live Renaissance music, traditional dances, and minstrel performances throughout the day.

Ticketing: Admission tickets are typically required for entry, with discounts available for seniors, children, and military personnel. Some festivals offer season passes for those who want to attend multiple weekends.

Before attending the Tampa Bay Area Renaissance Festival, it's a good idea to check the festival's official website for the latest information on dates, hours, ticketing, and any special events or themes for the year. Whether you're a history enthusiast, a fan of medieval fantasy, or simply looking for a fun and immersive experience, the Renaissance festival offers a magical journey back in time filled with entertainment, culture, and merriment.

103.Attend a Tampa Bay Rowdies soccer game.

Attending a Tampa Bay Rowdies soccer game is a thrilling experience for sports fans and a fantastic way to immerse yourself in the local sports culture of Tampa Bay, Florida. The Tampa Bay Rowdies are a professional soccer team that competes in the United Soccer League (USL), and they have a passionate fan base. Here's what you can typically expect when attending a Tampa Bay Rowdies soccer game:

Exciting Soccer Action: The Rowdies play high-energy soccer matches that are both competitive and entertaining. You can expect to witness skilled players, goal-scoring opportunities, and exciting moments throughout the game.

Al Lang Stadium: The team plays its home games at Al Lang Stadium, which is located in downtown St. Petersburg, across the bay from Tampa. The stadium offers great views of the field and the beautiful waterfront.

Tailgating: Many fans enjoy tailgating in the parking lots before the game. It's a fun tradition that allows supporters to socialize, enjoy food and drinks, and build excitement before kickoff.

Travel to Tampa Florida

Rowdies' Mob: The Rowdies' Mob is the official supporters' group of the team. They create a lively atmosphere at games with chants, songs, banners, and flags. Joining in with the Rowdies' Mob can enhance your game day experience.

Family-Friendly Environment: Rowdies games are family-friendly, making them an excellent outing for people of all ages. The atmosphere is typically lively but respectful.

Food and Beverages: Concession stands at the stadium offer a variety of food and beverage options, including classic stadium fare, snacks, and beverages.

Merchandise: You can purchase Rowdies merchandise at the stadium, including jerseys, scarves, hats, and other team gear.

Theme Nights: Some games may have special themes or promotions, such as fireworks nights, fan appreciation nights, or charity events. Check the team's schedule for details on upcoming theme nights.

Autographs and Fan Interaction: After some games, players may sign autographs or interact with fans. Check with the team or stadium for information on post-game events.

Tickets: Tickets can typically be purchased online through the team's official website or at the stadium box office. Prices may vary depending on seating and the opponent.

Parking: The stadium provides parking options for fans, and there are also nearby parking garages in downtown St. Petersburg.

Arrive Early: It's a good idea to arrive at the stadium early to ensure you have time to find parking, enjoy the pre-game atmosphere, and find your seats.

Attending a Tampa Bay Rowdies soccer game is a great way to enjoy a thrilling sporting event, bond with fellow fans, and support the local soccer community. Whether you're a die-hard soccer enthusiast or a casual sports fan, the Rowdies' games offer an exciting and memorable experience in the Tampa Bay area. Be sure to check the team's official website for the latest schedule, ticket information, and any special events or promotions.

104.Explore the Florida Holocaust Museum in nearby St. Petersburg.

The Florida Holocaust Museum in St. Petersburg, Florida, is a powerful and educational institution dedicated to preserving the memory of the Holocaust and promoting awareness of its history and lessons. Visiting the museum provides a sobering and informative experience that honors the victims of the Holocaust while emphasizing the importance of tolerance and human rights. Here's what you can typically expect when exploring the Florida Holocaust Museum:

Exhibitions: The museum features a series of thoughtfully curated exhibitions that tell the stories of Holocaust survivors, victims, and the historical context of the Holocaust. These exhibitions often include photographs, artifacts, documents, personal testimonies, and interactive displays.

Educational Programs: The museum offers educational programs and resources for visitors of all ages, including students, teachers, and community groups. These programs aim to promote understanding, empathy, and the prevention of hatred and discrimination.

The Anne Frank Center: Some Holocaust museums, including the Florida Holocaust Museum, may have a dedicated Anne Frank Center. This section of the museum focuses on the life and diary of Anne Frank, a Jewish girl who went into hiding during the Holocaust and whose diary became a symbol of hope and resilience.

Artifacts: The museum houses a collection of Holocaust artifacts, including personal items, clothing, concentration camp uniforms, and other objects that provide a tangible connection to the past.

Interactive Exhibits: Some exhibitions feature interactive elements that allow visitors to explore historical events and engage with survivor testimonies in a more immersive way.

Holocaust Memorial Center: Many Holocaust museums include a memorial center or garden dedicated to the memory of the victims. Visitors can pay their respects and reflect on the impact of the Holocaust.

Special Events: The museum may host special events, lectures, film screenings, and discussions related to the Holocaust and human rights issues. Check the museum's calendar for information on upcoming events.

Gift Shop: A museum gift shop typically offers books, educational materials, and other items related to the Holocaust and human rights.

Visitor Center: The museum's visitor center provides information about opening hours, admission, guided tours, and other practical details.

Guided Tours: Guided tours led by knowledgeable docents are often available for those who want a more in-depth exploration of the museum's exhibitions and history.

Accessibility: The museum is typically wheelchair accessible, and accommodations may be available for visitors with disabilities.

Photography: Visitors may be allowed to take photographs in certain areas of the museum, but it's important to respect any restrictions and guidelines regarding photography, especially in sensitive areas.

Visiting the Florida Holocaust Museum is a somber but essential experience that helps ensure that the memory of the Holocaust is never forgotten. It serves as a reminder of the consequences of hatred and discrimination and encourages visitors to actively promote tolerance, empathy, and social justice in their own lives. Before planning your visit, check the museum's official website for the latest information on hours of operation, admission fees, and any special exhibitions or events.

105.Go on a Tampa Bay wildlife photography tour.

A Tampa Bay wildlife photography tour is an excellent way for nature enthusiasts and photographers to capture the beauty of the region's diverse ecosystems and the stunning wildlife that inhabits them. These tours typically provide opportunities to observe and photograph a wide range of birds, mammals, reptiles, and other fauna in their natural habitats. Here's what you can generally expect on a wildlife photography tour in the Tampa Bay area:

Experienced Guides: Knowledgeable guides, often with expertise in local wildlife, lead the tours. They are well-versed in the behavior and habits of the animals you may encounter.

Scenic Locations: Tours take place in various natural settings, including wetlands, preserves, coastal areas, and parks known for their wildlife populations. Popular locations in the Tampa Bay area include Lettuce Lake Regional Park, the Florida Aquarium's Wild Dolphin Cruise, and Boyd Hill Nature Preserve.

Abundant Wildlife: The Tampa Bay region is home to a wide variety of wildlife, including waterfowl, wading birds, alligators, dolphins, manatees, and more. The tours aim to provide opportunities to observe and photograph these creatures up close.

Photography Tips: Guides often offer photography tips and advice on capturing the best shots. They may provide insights into composition, lighting, and camera settings to help you achieve stunning wildlife photographs.

Transportation: Depending on the tour, transportation may be provided to and from the wildlife photography locations. Some tours involve walking, while others use boats or vehicles for wildlife viewing.

Equipment Rentals: Some tour operators offer camera and lens rentals for participants who may not have specialized wildlife photography equipment.

Binoculars: Binoculars or spotting scopes may be available for participants to use for better wildlife observation.

Photography Ethics: Guides typically emphasize responsible wildlife photography and the importance of not disturbing or stressing the animals. Respect for the natural environment is a priority.

Seasonal Variations: Wildlife viewing opportunities can vary with the seasons, so it's a good idea to inquire about the best time of year for specific species.

Group Size: Tour groups are often kept small to ensure a more intimate and personalized experience.

Duration: Tours can vary in length, from a few hours to a full day, depending on the itinerary and the specific wildlife photography opportunities.

Environmental Education: Many tours also provide information about the local ecosystems, habitats, and conservation efforts, enhancing the educational aspect of the experience.

Before booking a wildlife photography tour in the Tampa Bay area, it's advisable to research different tour operators, read reviews, and inquire about the specific tour details, including availability, cost, and the types of wildlife you can expect to encounter. Whether you're a novice photographer or a seasoned pro, capturing the beauty of Tampa Bay's wildlife in its natural surroundings can be a rewarding and memorable experience.

106.Visit the Tampa Bay Automobile Museum.

The Tampa Bay Automobile Museum is a hidden gem for car enthusiasts and history buffs in the Tampa Bay area. Located in Pinellas Park, Florida, this museum showcases a unique collection of vintage automobiles from the early 20th century through the mid-20th century. It offers visitors a chance to explore the evolution of automotive engineering and design. Here's what you can typically expect when visiting the Tampa Bay Automobile Museum:

Rare and Vintage Cars: The museum houses a diverse collection of rare and vintage automobiles, including European and American models. These cars are meticulously maintained and often represent different eras and automotive innovations.

Educational Exhibits: Each car in the collection is displayed with informative panels that provide historical context, technical details, and interesting stories about the vehicle's history and significance.

Unique Engineering: One of the standout features of the museum is its focus on cars with unique and innovative engineering features. You'll find cars with front-wheel drive, rear-engine configurations, and other groundbreaking designs that were ahead of their time.

Interactive Displays: Some exhibits may feature interactive displays or hands-on activities that help visitors understand the mechanical and engineering principles behind these vintage automobiles.

Vintage Design: The museum's cars showcase the evolution of automotive design, from the elegance of classic luxury cars to the streamlined aesthetics of mid-century models.

Photography Opportunities: The museum provides excellent opportunities for photography, allowing visitors to capture the timeless beauty of these classic cars.

Guided Tours: Guided tours may be available, offering deeper insights into the history, engineering, and stories behind the cars in the collection.

Gift Shop: A museum gift shop typically offers automotive-themed merchandise, books, and memorabilia for visitors interested in taking home a souvenir.

Visitor Center: The museum's visitor center provides information about hours of operation, admission fees, and any special exhibitions or events.

Accessibility: The museum is often wheelchair accessible, and accommodations may be available for visitors with disabilities.

Private Events: Some museums offer event space for private functions, such as car clubs, weddings, or corporate events. Check with the museum for details if you're interested in hosting an event.

Educational Programs: The museum may offer educational programs for schools and groups, making it a valuable resource for learning about automotive history and technology.

Before planning your visit to the Tampa Bay Automobile Museum, be sure to check the museum's official website for the latest information on hours of operation, admission fees, and any special exhibitions or events. Whether you're a car enthusiast, a history buff, or simply curious about the evolution of automobiles, the museum provides a fascinating and enjoyable experience in the world of classic cars.

107. Go on a Tampa Bay Segway tour.

A Tampa Bay Segway tour is a fun and unique way to explore the city's attractions and landmarks while gliding effortlessly on a Segway personal transporter. These guided tours are typically led by knowledgeable guides who provide historical insights and interesting facts about the area. Here's what you can generally expect when going on a Segway tour in Tampa Bay:

Travel to Tampa Florida

Segway Training: Before the tour begins, participants are given a brief training session on how to operate a Segway safely. Segways are easy to learn to ride, and most people become comfortable with them quickly.

Choice of Tour Routes: Tour operators in Tampa Bay offer a variety of tour routes that may focus on different aspects of the city, such as historic districts, waterfront areas, or downtown highlights. Choose the tour that aligns with your interests.

Knowledgeable Guides: Experienced guides lead the tours and provide commentary along the way. They share historical anecdotes, fun facts, and local trivia about the sites you'll visit.

Scenic Stops: Segway tours often include stops at key landmarks, scenic viewpoints, and notable attractions. You'll have the opportunity to take photos and learn about the history of these sites.

Small Group Size: Tours are usually conducted in small groups to ensure a personalized and enjoyable experience. This also allows for more interaction with the guide.

Helmet and Safety Gear: Participants are provided with safety gear, including helmets, to ensure a safe and enjoyable ride.

Diverse Itineraries: Depending on the tour you choose, you may explore areas like downtown Tampa, the Tampa Riverwalk, historic Ybor City, Bayshore Boulevard, or other scenic spots.

Sunset Tours: Some tour operators offer evening or sunset Segway tours, which provide a different perspective of the city as it lights up for the night.

Private Tours: Private Segway tours may be available for those who prefer a more exclusive experience or want to customize the itinerary.

Age and Weight Restrictions: Tour operators typically have age and weight restrictions for participants. It's essential to check these requirements when booking.

Reservation: It's advisable to make reservations in advance, especially during peak tourist seasons, to secure your spot on the tour.

Accessibility: Segway tours are generally suitable for a wide range of participants, but it's essential to inquire about accessibility if you have specific mobility concerns.

Before booking a Tampa Bay Segway tour, be sure to check the tour operator's official website for the latest information on tour options, availability, pricing, and any special requirements. Riding a Segway is a fun and eco-friendly way to explore the city, and it offers a unique perspective on Tampa Bay's vibrant culture and attractions.

108.Explore the Ballast Point Park and Pier.

Ballast Point Park and Pier is a scenic waterfront destination located in the Ballast Point neighborhood of Tampa, Florida. It offers visitors a peaceful and picturesque place to enjoy the outdoors, go fishing, take a leisurely stroll, or simply relax by the water. Here's what you can expect when exploring Ballast Point Park and Pier:

Beautiful Waterfront Setting: The park is situated along the shores of Tampa Bay, providing stunning views of the bay and the skyline of Tampa. It's an ideal spot to watch the sunrise or sunset.

Fishing: The pier at Ballast Point is a popular spot for anglers. You can try your luck at catching a variety of fish, including snook, redfish, trout, and more. Be sure to bring your fishing gear and any required permits.

Picnicking: Ballast Point Park has picnic tables and shelters, making it a great place for a family picnic or a gathering with friends. You can enjoy your meal while taking in the waterfront views.

Playground: The park has a playground area for children, making it a family-friendly destination where kids can have fun and burn off some energy.

Walking and Jogging: There are paved paths and walkways throughout the park, providing a pleasant environment for a walk, jog, or leisurely stroll. The paths are lined with palm trees and offer shade in some areas.

Wildlife Viewing: Keep an eye out for local wildlife, including birds and marine life. Dolphins are occasionally spotted in the bay, and the park is home to a variety of bird species.

Photography: With its scenic views and serene atmosphere, Ballast Point Park and Pier are a photographer's paradise. Capture the beauty of the bay, the cityscape, and the park's natural surroundings.

Restrooms and Amenities: The park typically has restroom facilities, which can be convenient for visitors spending an extended period there.

Events and Gatherings: Some events, such as yoga classes, outdoor concerts, and community gatherings, may be held at Ballast Point Park. Check local event listings for any happenings during your visit.

Accessibility: The park is generally wheelchair accessible, with ramps and paved pathways.

Parking: Parking spaces are available at the park, making it convenient for visitors to access the waterfront area.

Hours: Ballast Point Park and Pier typically have set hours of operation, so it's a good idea to check in advance for their opening and closing times.

Ballast Point Park and Pier offer a tranquil escape from the hustle and bustle of the city and provide an opportunity to connect with nature and the beauty of Tampa Bay. Whether you're looking to enjoy outdoor activities, take in scenic views, or simply unwind by the water, this park is a delightful destination for residents and visitors alike.

109.Go on a fishing excursion in Tampa Bay.

Going on a fishing excursion in Tampa Bay is a fantastic way to experience the area's abundant marine life and enjoy the thrill of angling in one of Florida's premier fishing destinations. Tampa Bay offers a diverse range of fishing opportunities, from inshore and flats fishing to deep-sea and offshore adventures. Here's what you can typically expect when embarking on a fishing excursion in Tampa Bay:

Experienced Guides: Most fishing charters in Tampa Bay are led by experienced captains and guides who know the local waters, fishing spots, and the behavior of the fish species you're targeting. They are there to ensure a safe and successful fishing experience.

Variety of Fish Species: Tampa Bay is home to a wide variety of fish species, including snook, redfish, trout, tarpon, grouper, snapper, and more. The type of fish you can catch depends on the season and the location of your fishing excursion.

Inshore and Offshore Options: Tampa Bay offers both inshore and offshore fishing opportunities. Inshore fishing typically involves targeting species in the shallow waters, while offshore fishing ventures farther into the Gulf of Mexico for larger game fish.

All Equipment Provided: Most fishing charters provide all the necessary fishing gear, including rods, reels, bait, and tackle. You may also be provided with a fishing license, but it's a good idea to confirm this with the charter operator.

Customizable Trips: Many fishing charters offer customizable trips to cater to your preferences and skill level. Whether you're a novice angler or an experienced pro, there's an excursion suited to you.

Family-Friendly: Fishing in Tampa Bay can be a family-friendly activity. Some charters offer family packages and are equipped to accommodate children, ensuring an enjoyable experience for everyone.

Scenic Views: While on the water, you'll have the opportunity to enjoy the beautiful coastal scenery, spot wildlife like dolphins and seabirds, and even witness breathtaking sunsets.

Catch and Release: Some charters promote catch and release practices to preserve the local fish populations. Be sure to discuss your preferences with the captain.

Cleaning and Packaging: Depending on the charter, the crew may clean and package your catch for you to take home and enjoy.

Snacks and Refreshments: Some charters provide snacks and beverages, but it's a good idea to bring additional drinks and snacks, especially if you have dietary preferences.

Booking in Advance: Fishing charters in Tampa Bay can be in high demand, especially during peak fishing seasons. It's advisable to book your excursion in advance to secure your preferred date and time.

Weather Considerations: Keep in mind that weather conditions can impact fishing trips. Charters may need to be rescheduled or canceled if weather conditions are unsafe for fishing.

Tampa Bay is a year-round fishing destination, but the best time to fish for certain species may vary by season. Be sure to check with local fishing guides or charter operators for the most up-to-date information on fishing conditions and availability. Whether you're a novice angler looking for a fun day on the water or a seasoned fisherman seeking a big catch, Tampa Bay has something to offer every fishing enthusiast.

110. Visit the Glazer Children's Museum.

The Glazer Children's Museum is a vibrant and interactive educational destination located in downtown Tampa, Florida. Designed for children and families, this museum offers a wide range of exhibits and activities that promote learning through play and exploration. Here's what you can expect when visiting the Glazer Children's Museum:

Hands-On Exhibits: The museum features a variety of hands-on and interactive exhibits that cater to children of all ages. These exhibits cover various topics, including science, art, health, and the environment.

Art and Creativity: Children can unleash their creativity in art studios and workshops. They can engage in painting, sculpting, and other artistic activities, fostering their imagination and self-expression.

Science and Technology: Discover interactive exhibits that introduce young minds to the wonders of science and technology. From experimenting with simple machines to exploring the principles of physics, kids can engage in educational play.

Health and Wellness: Some exhibits focus on promoting healthy living and well-being. Children can learn about the human body, nutrition, and the importance of exercise through fun and engaging activities.

Outdoor Play: The museum often includes outdoor play areas where children can burn off energy while enjoying physical activities.

Educational Programming: Check the museum's schedule for special events, workshops, and programs. They may offer themed activities, guest speakers, and educational opportunities.

Birthday Parties and Group Visits: The Glazer Children's Museum is a popular destination for birthday parties and group outings. They often offer packages for private celebrations and educational field trips.

Cafeteria and Gift Shop: The museum may have an on-site cafeteria or snack area where you can grab a bite to eat. There's also usually a gift shop with educational toys and souvenirs.

Accessibility: The museum is generally designed to be accessible to visitors with disabilities, with features like ramps and wheelchair-accessible restrooms.

Membership: Consider becoming a member of the museum for discounts on admission, special events, and exclusive access.

Hours of Operation: Check the museum's official website for information about hours of operation, admission prices, and any special events or exhibitions.

The Glazer Children's Museum provides an engaging and educational environment where children can learn through play and exploration. It's an ideal destination for families, school groups, and anyone interested in fostering creativity and curiosity in young minds. When planning your visit, be sure to check the museum's website or contact them directly for the most up-to-date information on exhibits and programs.

Conclusion

Tampa, Florida, is a rich tapestry that spans centuries and reflects the city's evolution from a remote outpost to a vibrant and diverse metropolis. From its early Native American inhabitants and Spanish explorers to its pivotal role in the American Civil War, Tampa's history has been shaped by numerous cultural, economic, and social influences.

The city's growth was significantly accelerated by the arrival of the railroad and the establishment of its deepwater port, which facilitated trade and commerce. The cigar industry and the influx of Cuban immigrants in the late 19th and early 20th centuries left an indelible mark on Tampa's cultural heritage.

Tampa's history also includes a period of booming industry, with the rise of the phosphate and cigar industries, as well as its status as a military hub during both World Wars. The mid-20th century brought suburban expansion, the growth of tourism, and the development of a thriving business community.

Tampa's more recent history is characterized by urban revitalization, a diverse population, and a strong focus on cultural enrichment. The city has become a hub for arts, sports, and technology, contributing to its reputation as a dynamic and forward-thinking place.

While this history overview provides a glimpse into Tampa's past, it's important to remember that the city continues to evolve, welcoming new generations of residents and visitors. Tampa's history is not just a story of the past; it's an ongoing narrative of progress, diversity, and the enduring spirit of a city that remains deeply connected to its roots while embracing the challenges and opportunities of the future.

If you enjoyed, please leave a 5-star Amazon Review

To get a free list of people who knows publishing top places to travel all around the world, click this link
https://bit.ly/peoplewhoknowtravel

Travel to Tampa Florida

References

Rcsprinter123, CC BY-SA 3.0 <https://creativecommons.org/licenses/by-sa/3.0>, via Wikimedia Commons
https://pixabay.com/photos/abstract-american-background-1238657/

Printed in Dunstable, United Kingdom